The Fighting Kukri

This training manual is respectively dedicated to my mentor and friend,
W. Hoch Hochheim, whose guidance has always kept my focus
within the world of reality.

The Fighting Kukri

Illustrated Lessons on the Gurkha Combat Knife

Dwight C. McLemore

PALADIN PRESS ■ BOULDER, COLORADO

Other Paladin titles by Dwight C. McLemore:
Advanced Bowie Techniques
Bowie and Big-Knife Fighting System
The Fighting Gladiator
The Fighting Staff
The Fighting Sword
The Fighting Tomahawk
The Fighting Tomahawk, Vol. II
The Fighting Tomahawk: The Video

The Fighting Kukri:
Illustrated Lessons on the Gurkha Combat Knife
by Dwight C. McLemore

Copyright © 2012 by Dwight C. McLemore

ISBN 13: 978-1-61004-572-8
Printed in the United States of America

Published by Paladin Press, a division of
Paladin Enterprises, Inc.,
P.O. Box 1307
Boulder, Colorado 80306 USA
+1.303.443.7250

Direct inquiries and/or orders to the above address.

Visit our website at www.paladin-press.com.

Warning

Misuse of the information and techniques in this book could result in serious injury or death. The author, publisher, and distributor of this text disclaim any liability from damage or injuries of any type that a reader or user of the information may incur. The techniques should never be attempted or practiced without the direct supervision of a qualified weapons instructor. Moreover, it is the reader's responsibility to research and comply with all local, state, and federal laws and regulations pertaining to possession, carry, and use of edged weapons. The text is for *academic study only*.

Contents

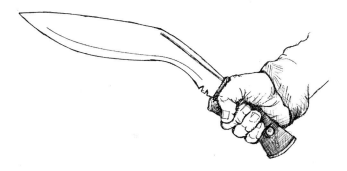

The Fighting Kukri

The Fighting Kukri

Introduction

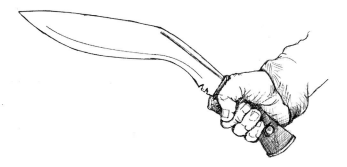

This text is not a stand-alone, all-inclusive dissertation on how to fight with the historic kukri. I am not a kukri master, nor is it my intention to duplicate the techniques of any specific martial system that has adopted the kukri as its signature weapon. This is a training support package that is simply my take on how the weapon could be used within a fighting scenario.

The text does not strictly adhere to the traditionally sequential and progressive approach of most training manuals. Rather, it is a sprinkling of history, fighting approaches, and training exercises on cutting, thrusting, blocking, and the associated movement of a potential kukri fight. In writing this text, I have made the assumption that the reader has a working knowledge of edged weapons from some martial system. I have included terms and concepts that compose a training language that I've used over the years. I have to admit to borrowing a variety of geometric elements from several martial disciplines of both East and West that are easily adaptable to the kukri. I have not hesitated to mix both modern and historical concepts that inspired me during my exploration of this unique weapon.

While I have tried to keep all this information reasonably straightforward and tied to the reality of the modern world, you will find that I have illustrated many techniques with opponents squared off in one-on-one scenarios. These should be viewed as an artistic means of clarity to depict a training point, not a naïve belief in some dueling scenario. While I am fully aware of the unlikely possibility of squared-off, one-on-one fights occurring today, they do provide a vehicle to illustrate medium-range techniques that are often the starting point for close-quarter combat.

Like the bowie knife, the kukri is a historic weapon that is as much a part of myth and folklore as it is reality. To fully understand how it is used, one must delve into the history of its country of origin, its design, and its applications. That said, many of the sidebars in this book contain historical elements that will help enhance instructors' training presentations. The text is for martial artists, fight directors of stage and screen, historical reenactors, and those individuals who make their living in the profession of arms.

Note: There are several spellings in use today for the kukri, including *kurkuri* (a phonetic spelling that is closest to the way the people of Nepal pronounce the term), *khukuri*, and *khukri*. I have chosen to use the standard spelling most familiar to a Western audience.

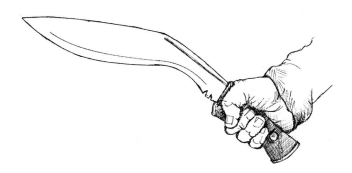

How to Use This Manual

The Fighting Kukri is composed of three books. Book 1 is a compilation of various fighting and training concepts I have used over the years. Again, this is simply my take on some of the aspects of edged weapon training. It is a synthesis of concepts that I addressed in *The Fighting Tomahawk, Vol. II*, *The Fighting Staff*, and *The Fighting Sword*. If you are familiar with these, or if you are secure in your personal martial system, simply move on to the Training Notes in Book 2 and Engagement Scenarios in Book 3. I want you to think of this manual as yours! Take it to the training hall, make notes on the pages, and use it as a memory aid for your kukri instruction.

BOOK 1

FUNDAMENTAL TRAINING CONCEPTS

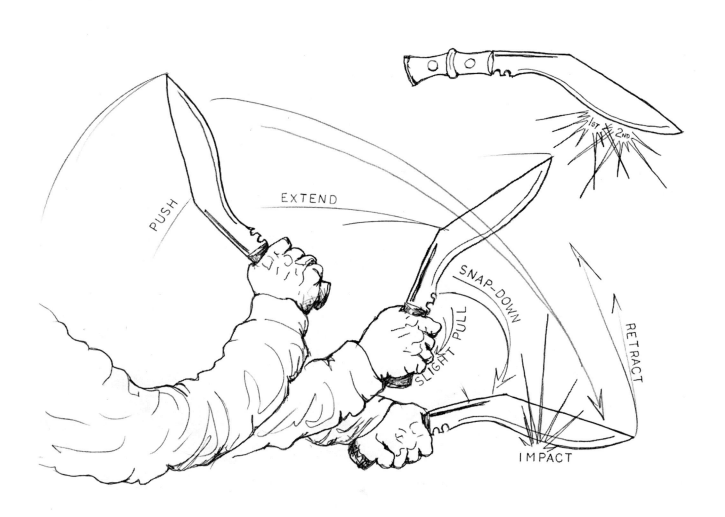

Chapter 1

History and Design of the Kukri

The kukri just may be one of the oldest utility/combat knives in existence today. It has come to be recognized as the national weapon of Nepal and has been associated with the British Army's Gurkha brigade since its creation. The knife is of humble origins, with hundreds of variations made by the Kami blacksmith caste of Nepal and in some locations in India.

The true origin of the kukri design has been lost to the centuries. Some historians believe that the downward sloping point can be traced back to Alexander the Great's invasion of the Punjab in 326 BCE, when the region was exposed to the *makaira* and *kopis* carried by his troops. Others see relationships to the Iberian *falcata*. There is also the possibility that the weapon may be an evolution of the *kora* sword of the same geographic area as Nepal. The design of the *aitihasik*, considered the original kukri, was introduced in 1768 during King Prithvi Narayan Shah's war of unification of the area that would later become Nepal. This version of the kukri is depicted in many of the illustrations in this manual.

The bottom line on the origins of the kukri's distinctive design is that, like the American bowie knife, it is elusive and shrouded in myth and legend. The kukri comes in a variety of blade shapes and sizes that can be grouped into four representatives types, each associated with one of the tribal cultures of Nepal. A modern kukri may not have been physically made in one of the four traditional areas, but its design still may be based on one of the four traditional types.

The long, thin-bladed *hanshee* and *sirupati* versions come from western Nepal, while the robust, deep-bellied *budhume* and *bhojpure* originate in the east. There are other historic tribal designs, but they are too numerous to accurately designate who made what. Figures 1 and 2 depict four common blade designs. Figure 3 depicts a generic government contract design that is still sold today. My favorite is the

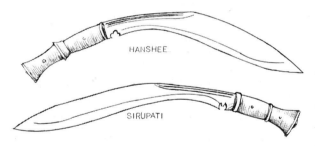

Figure 1

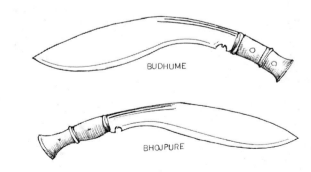

Figure 2

The Fighting Kukri

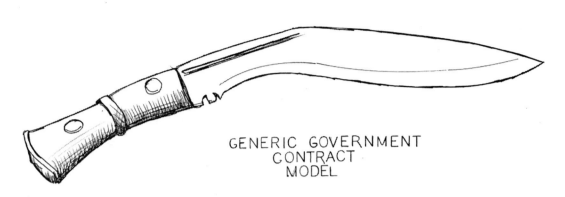

GENERIC GOVERNMENT
CONTRACT
MODEL

Figure 3

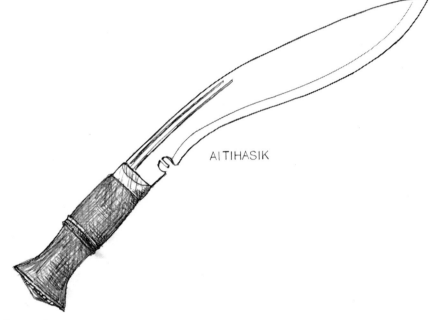

AITIHASIK

Figure 4

historic *aitihasik* of the eighteenth century depicted in Figure 4.

KUKRI DESIGN SPECIFICATIONS

Figure 5 illustrates the various parts of the generic kukri that we have come to know today. As I mentioned, these specifications may vary considerably, depending on when and where the knife was made. Here are the basic terms we will use throughout this manual.

The Edge
This portion of the kukri blade is composed of three parts: the cho, the recurve, and the belly. The belly of the blade is the primary sharpened cutting edge, while the recurve may only have a beveled false edge. This is not an absolute rule but rather a generic view, not unlike some designs that actually have a false edge on the lower spine.

The cho is the small notch on the edge side of the blade near the handle. It has a variety of religious and functional purposes, depending on the cultural and tribal origins of the design. The true meaning has been lost in the clouds of time. Some say it represents the Nepali symbol for the sun or moon, while others believe it is the footprint of the sacred cow of the Hindus. The more religious believe it represents the sex organs of the gods Kali or Shiva, whereas utilitarian experts claim the notch to be a blood drip channel or substitute guard. I believe this notch is probably more folklore than functional, not unlike the Spanish notch or brass strip found on some nineteenth-century knives. Today, it is probably more decorative than anything else. It certainly looks cool.

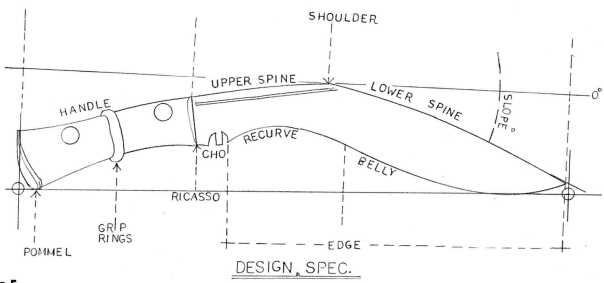

Figure 5

The Ricasso

This is the unsharpened portion of the blade closest to the handle. This is another of those Western terms that over time has found its way into the vocabulary to describe an Eastern object. Go figure!

The Handle

In addition to the recurve blade, the handle of the kukri is also unique. Most have one or two grip rings that, while very functional, may have religious meanings. No expert today seems to have the same answer on this. The pommel is usually heavy and helps provide balance to the point-heavy blade.

The Spine

The upper spine is the portion of the blade that extends from the ricasso to the shoulder of the blade. It is characterized by the deep fuller that runs the length of the upper spine. A common myth identifies fullers as "blood grooves" that supposedly let the blood drain away from the handle. While a fuller might actually function in this manner, its real utility is to reduce weight and increase the strength of the blade.

The lower spine composes that unique downward sloping curve for which the kukri is best known. With a traditional kukri, the degree of slope depends on the tribal area where it was made. On a modern version, the degree depends on the traditional pattern upon which it is based.

Chapter 2

Types and Language of the Cuts

Since most experts see the role of the kukri is that of a cutting weapon or tool, it is here where we will begin our exploration. The unique downward slope of the blade, along with the convex belly, give the weapon a point-heavy feel that uses gravity to effect powerful, accurate cuts. The kukri design can also accommodate effective thrusts, but some training is necessary to adjust to the point-down aspect. We will address thrusts later, but for now we need to examine the types of cuts that can be used in conjunction with this kukri manual.

THE CUTS

There are two basic methods for delivering kukri cuts: the long strike and the short strike. The long strike is performed with one hand and used for cutting targets at medium range or arm's length. It is ideal for those situations where you want to maintain some distance between you and the opponent, as depicted in Figure 6. Often, these cuts are followed with a follow-on cut from a different position or angle.

The short strike, illustrated in Figure 7, is delivered in those situations where the opponent is very close or there is no space to accommodate the more expansive long strike. The elbow is usually bent during delivery, and power-assist techniques are sometimes used to push through an opponent's defense.

Figure 6

SHORT STRIKE

Figure 7

Here are the four basic cuts that work with both long and short strike delivery techniques.

The Standard Cut

Figure 8 illustrates aspects of delivering a standard cut with a long strike. In this example, the weapon is moved into position and launched from the high line. The arm is slightly flexed and extended out into a descending arc to impact into and through the target. There is a slight pull just before or during impact, depicted in the lower left of Figure 8. The grip for the standard cut is the universal grip seen in Figure 9. Today, as in the past, few altercations take place at medium range. The onset may begin at arm's length, but things quickly get to "in your face" range, so the arc of the strike needs to be shortened to accommodate the close quarters. Here is where the short strike comes into play.

Types and Language of the Cuts

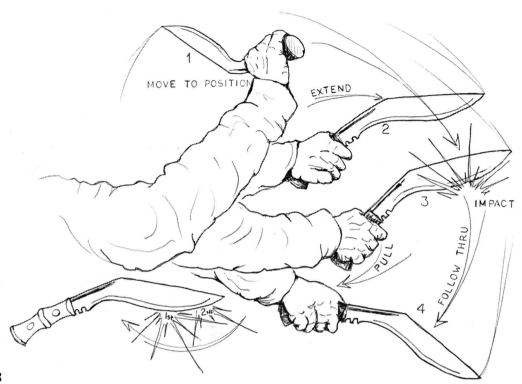

Figure 8

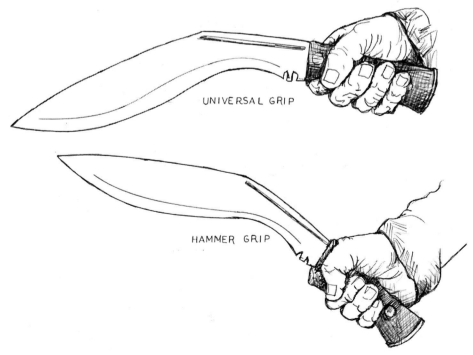

Figure 9

The Chop

The chop drives the belly of the blade through a variety of structural, muscular, and vascular targets. This is a cleaving action that penetrates the target, usually requiring the weapon to be retracted back along the same line of entry. It can be delivered along angles to targets at both medium and close range, using both long and short strike delivery techniques. The chop is initiated with the same pushing action as the standard cut, but while holding the kukri in the hammer grip depicted in Figure 9. The blade is presented roughly at the same angle throughout the arc of the swing. Just short of impact, a slight pull is initiated that violently snaps the belly down and into the target, as seen in Figure 10.

The Draw Cut

This technique is performed as a follow-through to either a chop or standard cut. The most common targets are vascular or organs protected by heavy clothing. The action begins with a chop into the target area. As the belly achieves the penetration depth, the weapon is pulled back along a line that draws the edge through additional targets, as illustrated in Figure 11.

The Snap Cut

This cut is executed with a hammer grip, where the blade is pushed out horizontally with the wrist locked and the edge at an approximate 45-degree angle. As the target is neared, the wrist is unlocked and the point is snapped down and forward into the target area, as seen in Figure 12. The snap cut is often used with normal, straight-bladed knives to cut distraction targets such as the forehead and hands. The heavier blade of the kukri allows for deeper penetrating wounds against structural and organ targets.

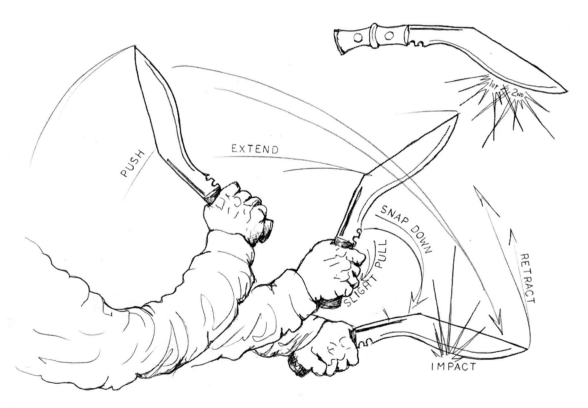

Figure 10

Types and Language of the Cuts

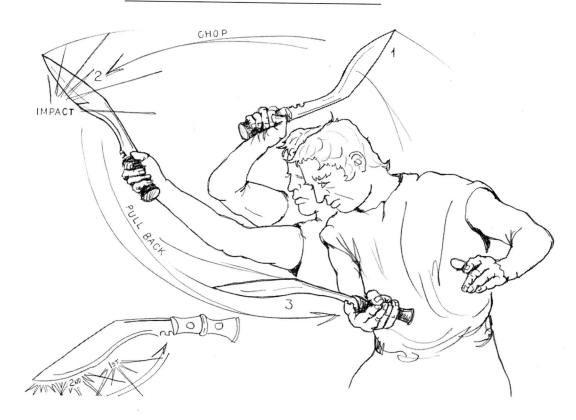

Figure 11

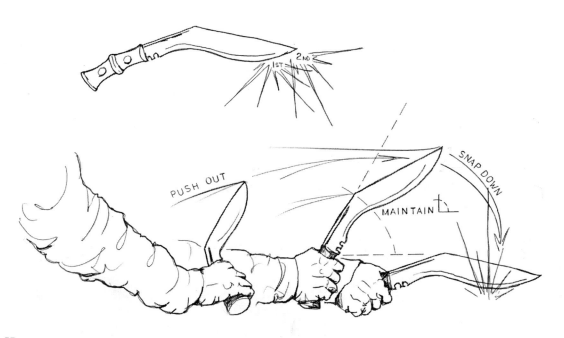

Figure 12

15

ANGLES OF ATTACK AND THE LANGUAGE OF CUTTING PATTERNS

The concept of using geometric angles to teach cutting techniques is very old. This often takes the form of diagrams and charts, a genre of training aids that have appeared in fighting books as far back as the 1500s. (They were particularly popular in fencing manuals of the sixteenth through nineteenth centuries.) These angles of attack serve as a point of reference to teach how to engage specific targets in the high, middle, and low-line target areas.

Figure 13 depicts one of these wall charts that I've used for several years. It is a modification of Donald Walker's diagram for broadsword included in his 1840 text *Defensive Exercises*. I enlarged it into a full-size human silhouette chart and use it to teach new students the "language" of the cuts. I see no reason why it will not work just as well for the kukri. Figure 14 illustrates a more detailed view of the angles in relation to high, middle, and low-line target areas that we will use to examine specific targets.

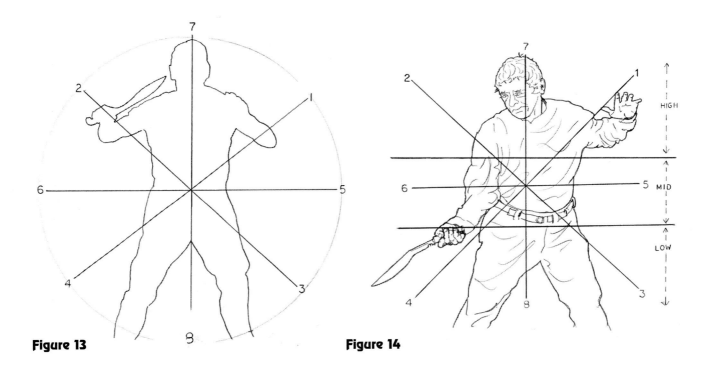

Figure 13

Figure 14

Types and Language of the Cuts

RELATIONSHIPS BETWEEN ANGLES AND TARGETS

Throughout this manual, we will be identifying targets using terms derived from the 2006 Paladin Press publication *Contemporary Knife Targeting* by Christopher Grosz and Michael Janich. Specifically, the definitions on pages 20–21 of distraction, vascular, nervous system, organ, structural, and muscular targets should be reviewed.

The High Line

As can be seen in Figure 15, the high-line area is impacted by angles 1, 2, and 7. These are descending cuts on both the left and right of the centerline. The targets are essentially the same for either side. Angle 7 encompasses the structural targets on the top of the skull and distraction targets such as the eyes, nose, and mouth. The temple offers another structural target that can stun or render an opponent unconscious. The neck and throat are key vascular targets that can disrupt the flow of blood to the heart and brain, rendering the opponent unconscious. Another structural target along angles 1 and 2 is the ball joint of the shoulder, which, when impacted, can affect the opponent's ability to move his arm.

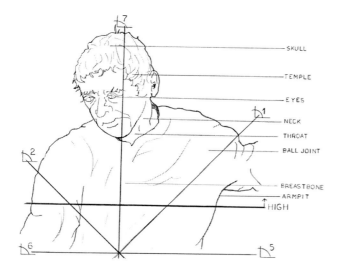

Figure 15

The Middle Line

All of the attack angles cross at the center of this area. Organ targets such as the heart, lungs, and abdomen can be cut from any of the angles. The structural targets of the hands and forearms provide opportunities for distraction or affecting movement. Delivery can take the form of ascending or descending cuts. Figure 16 provides a generic view of the targets in the midline area.

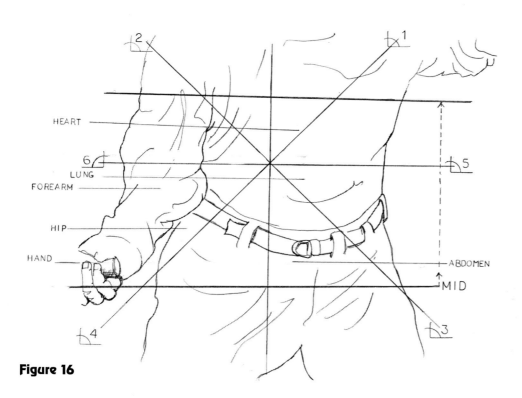

Figure 16

The Low Line

This area, illustrated in Figure 17, is impacted primarily from angles 3, 4, and 8. Attacks to the low line are usually ascending cuts that impact into the groin or inner leg at arterial targets such as the femoral and iliac arteries. The knee, calf, and their associated connective tissues are primary structural targets at the low line.

Note: For the sake of brevity, I only address targets that are presented when facing the opponent "inside the box." Those targets "outside the box" will be addressed in the engagement scenarios in Book Three.

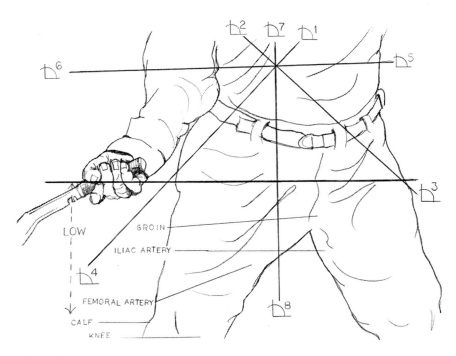

Figure 17

THE THEORY OF INSIDE AND OUTSIDE THE BOX

Another concept I took from historical fencing is that of "inside the box" and "outside the box." This concept has been addressed in almost every martial arts book I have written, so if you are already familiar with it, you can move on to the next chapter.

Basically, we are talking about the relationship between you and your opponent in terms of distance, time, position, and weapons involved. When you and your opponent face each other in a frontal position, there is an imaginary box comprised of his torso, head, and arms. When you are in this position, as seen on the left of Figure 18, you are considered to be inside the box. This is a very dangerous place to be, because anything you do or your opponent does is likely to be

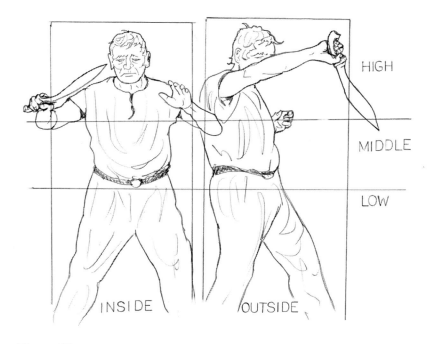

Figure 18

observed. If your opponent is armed with two weapons, he has the advantage of being able to engage you from almost any angle. When you attack from inside the box, you will almost invariably receive an immediate counterattack. This is not to say one cannot attack from this position—just be aware of the danger.

The drawing on the right in Figure 18 depicts an opponent as seen from outside the box. You are essentially outside his weapon arm. This position is desirable because the opponent must change his position to defend or attack.

Another aspect that must be considered in this discussion is when the opponent is using a two-handed weapon, such as the staff in Figure 19. Note that the area of your opponent's lead hand and leg is considered outside and the area of his rear hand and leg inside. The staff is particularly dangerous because any attacks you make when you are inside can be countered from both above and below. The opponent can launch rapid descending attacks from outside and follow immediately with quick low-line attacks from inside. Bottom line: an opponent armed with a staff can defend against most of your attacks.

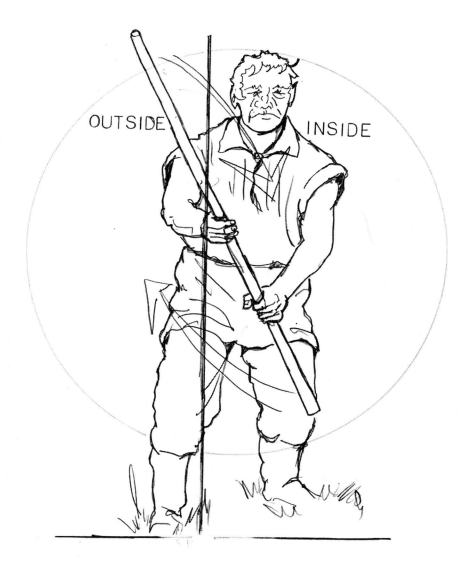

Figure 19

Chapter 3

Guards, Stances, Blocks, and Parries

Historically, the guard has been viewed as a ready posture that has both offensive and defensive potential. From the defensive view, it can be used to block, parry, or evade an incoming attack. Offensively, guards have historically been used as initial and final positions that compose the path that certain cuts/thrusts take into or through a target. Personally, I think this type of guard linking is primarily for sword training. This approach is fine if you have trained up with it, but I've found that it detracts from the instinctual and impromptu nature associated with smaller knife-like weapons.

THE GUARDS

I see the guards as those positions that are moved to and passed through to accomplish blocking, parrying, or launching attacks. The term "stance" is often used in combination with the guards, depending on which leg is positioned closest to the opponent. When the lead leg is on the same side as the weapon hand, it is considered to be the strong-side forward stance. When the lead leg and empty opposite hand are on the same side, it is referred to as a weak-side forward stance. Figure 20 depicts these aspects of the stance.

To help understand the defensive aspect of the guards, we need to introduce a training icon to depict incoming cut/thrust attacks. Figure 21 is the cutting angle pattern that we discussed in chapter 2, where *you* are delivering the strikes against the person in the illustration. In Figure 22, the perspective is reversed—the *opponent* in the figure is delivering a variety of cuts toward the viewer. Figure 23 represents incoming

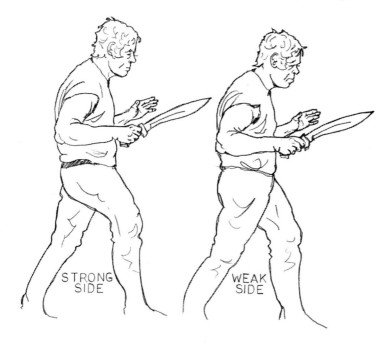

STRONG SIDE

WEAK SIDE

Figure 20

The Fighting Kukri

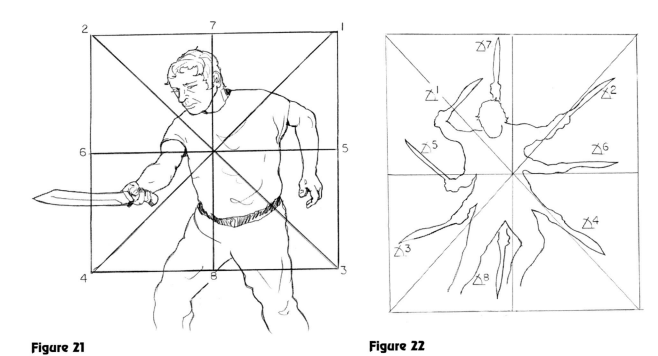

Figure 21

Figure 22

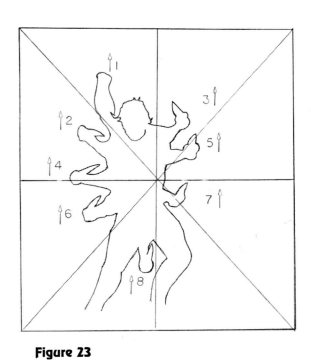

Figure 23

22

thrusts. You will find these diagrams on some of the illustrations in this text to represent the "cue" that one might receive during attacks at high, middle, and low-line areas. They are composed from photo mosaics that reveal the change of the shape or silhouette of the weapon as it appears during attacks from the different angles.

Like other martial systems, I have designated three guards to defeat specific incoming attack angles.

Figure 24

Figure 25

The Middle Guard

This guard can be used with either strong- or weak-side stances. The blade is held along the centerline at waist height, with the point aimed at the opponent's midsection, as depicted in Figure 24. The empty hand can be held parallel to the weapon or with a slight chamber at the elbow. The point here is to not extend the empty hand too far out, where it can become a target. As depicted in the icon on the right of the figure, this guard is effective for countering most high and middle-line attack angles. Offensively, this guard is an excellent launch point for thrusts. With most cuts, however, it may be necessary to move the weapon into a striking position, which could cue the opponent to your intentions. If an attack comes from the low line, it may be necessary to use footwork and drop the point from this guard to defend against it.

The High Guard

Figure 25 depicts a generic version of the high guard. The weapon arm and empty hand are raised to form a triangle shape in front of the face. As with the middle guard, the empty hand should be retracted back a bit to prevent exposure to attack. This guard is effective against most high-line attack angles, but it leaves the low and middle lines vulnerable.

The Fighting Kukri

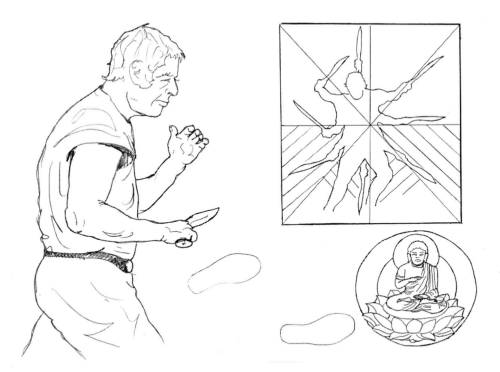

Figure 26

The Low Guard

Here the weapon is held low in the midline area, as illustrated in Figure 26. The empty hand is pulled back into a chamber with the hand positioned slightly in front of the chest. The weapon hand is moved across the abdomen to a position under the empty hand. This guard is used to defend against attacks to the low line; it is also particularly effective for delivering rapid snap cuts to the opponent's head, hands, or groin area.

BLOCKING AND PARRYING

The primary defensive applications off a guard take the form of either a block or parry. Basically, a block involves stopping the momentum of an incoming strike. It can be executed with either one or two hands, and a counterattack can be launched afterward.

Figure 27 illustrates a one-handed block against a horizontal cut. The unique recurve of the kukri is the strongest part of the blade and therefore the best impact zone. If the block is too high on the belly of the blade, the opponent's weapon can slide off and

The Martial Aspect of Guards Seen in Buddhist Mandalas

A few years back, I did some research on the influence of Eastern martial arts in Buddhist doctrine and vice versa. What I found fascinating was how many martial techniques had become enshrined within a spiritual concept. One of the best examples can be seen in the mandala illustrations of China, Japan, and the Indian subcontinent, of which Nepal is a part.

The mystical, ritual positions of the Vajradhatu Mahamandala are identical to the defensive ready positions and gestures discussed here. Look at the tutelary deities or Bodhisattvas in the lower right of Figures 24, 25, and 26 and note how their positions resemble the guards. I've added these only as a point of interest and a possible indicator of the age of these techniques.

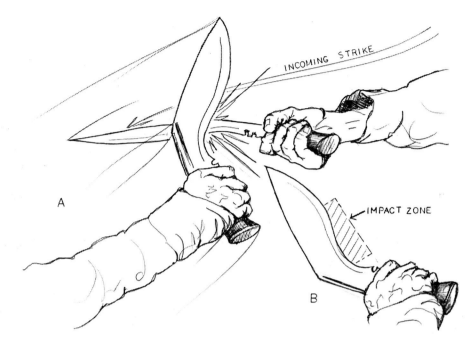

Figure 27

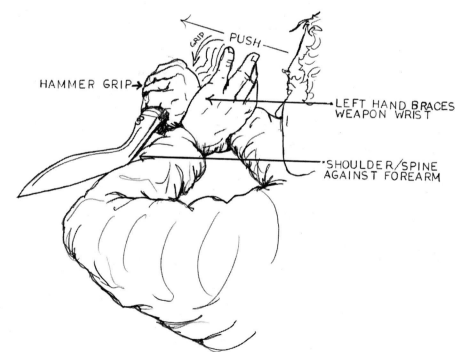

Figure 28

more or less blow through your guard, affecting a cut.

The block can also be executed with two hands, as depicted in Figure 28. Here the left hand is positioned behind the weapon hand to support the upper spine. This positioning forms a good defensive triangle that adds additional stopping power to the block.

The parry consists of a deflection of the incoming strike that sets aside the opponent's blade and provides the opportunity for counterattack. It is most effective when combined with footwork that takes the body out of the line of attack. Figure 29 depicts a standard method of parrying, which involves cutting into the strike, deflecting the blade with the upper part of the recurve, and following through with a counterattack. The parry can also be accomplished with the lower portion of the spine, as illustrated in Figure 30. Here the kukri is pulled across and into a strike with the lower spine, not unlike the back-cut techniques associated with the bowie knife.

Before going ahead with the training flow for blocks, parries, and their counterattacks, we need to examine the concepts of footwork and movement.

The Fighting Kukri

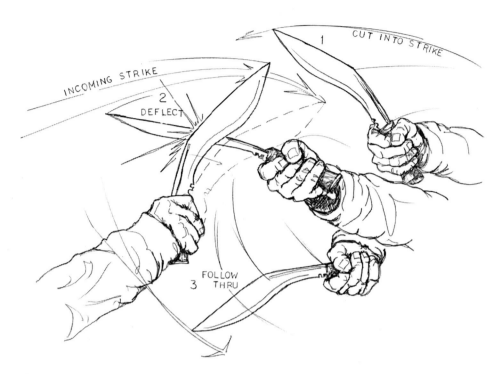

Figure 29

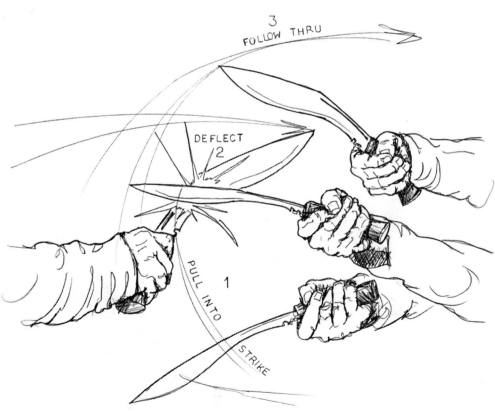

Figure 30

Chapter 4

Basic Stepping Footwork and Movement

Figures 31 and 32 represent the generic stepping patterns that I have selected for use with the kukri. I am not going to go into my rationale for selecting these particular patterns other than to suggest that you read Letters 3 and 21 of my text *The Fighting Tomahawk, Volume II* to see how the aspects of terrain, weather, tread, gait, and footwear can impact on the aspects of distance, time, and position when engaging an opponent. Briefly here are three conclusions that I arrived at:

- Stepping and striking usually will occur simultaneously, whether moving forward or backward.
- Footwork is the vehicle to affect changes in distance, time, and position associated with creating openings for attack during the onset, hand-on-hand, and follow-on aspect of any engagement.
- Tread, gait, and balance work hand-in-hand when determining the "messages" of the opponent and environment in most engagements.

Now let's look at the stepping patterns in more detail.

STEP FORWARD AND STEP BACK

This pattern is sometimes referred to as an advancing or retreating step. I've also seen it identified as a gathering step. It is used when you are facing an opponent and there is a tactical need to approach or withdraw in and out of the engagement

range. It is very effective in avoiding vertical strikes from above or below. Figure 31 provides a visualization of the linear nature of this pattern.

To step forward, begin with a strong-side forward stance and take a normal walking stride with the lead foot. Almost simultaneously, step forward with the rear foot and end up back in a strong-side forward position. This completes one step forward. To step back from a strong-side forward stance, take a normal walking step backward with the rear foot. As soon as the rear foot touches down, step back with the lead foot into a strong-side forward position. This completes one step backward.

Practice this stepping sequence slowly at first, focusing on feeling the ground with your feet. Next, practice taking two to three forward steps one after another; then repeat it stepping backward. You will find it interesting to notice how much distance can be covered with this erratic stepping rhythm. Finally, experiment with these stepping techniques at full speed. Have your training partner execute them while you observe. Notice the steps have a sort of halting rhythm. Consider how observing this rhythm could be used to fix, attack, or disrupt an opponent's intentions.

STEP LEFT AND STEP RIGHT

During any engagement, the need may arise to sidestep to avoid a kick, strike, thrust, or an opponent's mad rush. This stepping pattern takes the body

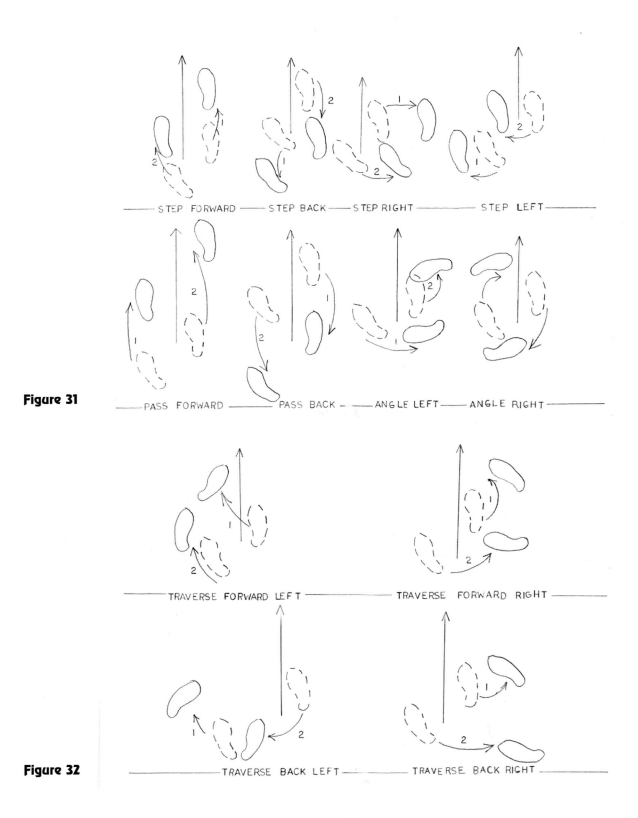

Figure 31

STEP FORWARD — STEP BACK — STEP RIGHT — STEP LEFT

PASS FORWARD — PASS BACK — ANGLE LEFT — ANGLE RIGHT

TRAVERSE FORWARD LEFT — TRAVERSE FORWARD RIGHT

Figure 32

TRAVERSE BACK LEFT — TRAVERSE BACK RIGHT

off the centerline to the left or right, as illustrated in Figure 31. The feet and legs maintain their frontal orientation, with only the head and shoulders shifting orientation to accommodate any follow-on action by the opponent.

To step right, begin by moving the lead foot approximately 12–20 inches to the right of the original position. As it touches down, move the rear foot over and across the centerline to the right, which will take you back into the strong-side forward position. To step left, move the left rear foot across the centerline approximately 12–20 inches. As soon as it touches down, move the right foot over and across the center and back into the original strong-side forward stance.

The distance of these steps will depend on one's natural gait needed to maintain balance, as well as the condition of the surface you are moving over. That said, experiment with these on the side of a hill or some other slope, being aware of how far the initiating foot can move to maintain balance. As with the other steps, practice this at different speeds and observe the rhythm.

PASS FORWARD AND PASS BACK

This pattern is used whenever you have to cover a lot of ground to avoid a strike or when an opponent is closing the distance between you. This is basically a walking stride or pace where one foot passes the other. Figure 31 depicts a single stride of this technique; however, it can be repeated as many times as needed to avoid or initiate an attack.

To pass forward from a strong-side forward stance, begin by moving the rear foot forward and past the lead leg. As the rear foot touches down, move the original lead leg past the original rear leg and end up back in a strong-side forward stance. This is considered one pass forward. On the pass back, move the lead leg back to a position to the rear of the original rear leg. As it touches down, move the original rear leg back to a position past the original lead leg. This is considered one pass backward.

ANGLE LEFT AND ANGLE RIGHT

These steps are used when there is not a lot of room to maneuver or at very, very close range. The angling is often accompanied by violent rotation of the hips and trunk to avoid being hit. This pattern can be used in conjunction with other patterns to create further openings or get out of the way of an incoming attack. These are particularly effective when an opponent has closed and is more or less in your face, requiring the use of elbows and shoulders to lever into a favorable position.

Angle left is executed by swinging the rear foot around to the right rear while simultaneously pivoting on the heel or toe of the lead foot. Angle right involves swinging the lead foot around to your right. As the lead foot stops, the rear foot swings around to a position parallel to the centerline. This footwork is illustrated at the bottom right of Figure 31.

TRAVERSE FORWARD AND BACK

There will always be circumstances that will require you to move out on an angle to the opponent across the centerline. This is true if you are trying to get outside the box to acquire an opening.

Traverse forward left begins by stepping forward and across the centerline with the right lead foot and following with the left, as depicted in the upper left of Figure 32. Traverse forward right begins by stepping around and to the left of the centerline and then swinging the left rear foot around to the left rear. Traverse back left begins by swinging the lead right foot back and around across the centerline to a stop behind the left rear foot. As the lead foot stops, the rear swings out and to the side into the original strong-side forward position. Traverse back right involves stepping away from the centerline to the right, then swinging the left foot around back to the original position.

Before we return to the business of cutting, let's take a look at the "rhythm" of the fight and its application to the aspects of distance, time, and position.

Chapter 5

Tactical Elements and Rhythm of the Fight

In the latter part of 2008, I worked on a manuscript titled *The Sword of Wood*, which was to be my take on the 1570 German treatise *Gründtliche Beschreibung der Kunst des Fechten* by Joachim Meyer. The focus of Meyer's book was the German training sword called the *dussack*. In his text, Meyer breaks down an engagement or altercation into three parts that are applicable to a variety of long and short weapons. I have modified these parts to provide a presentation format for the various kukri techniques and engagement scenarios included in this manual.

They are as applicable today as they were in the sixteenth century.

THE ONSET

This is the phase of the engagement where two opponents move into striking range of their particular weapon. This is not unlike the Japanese sword concept of "moon on water" put forth by sixteenth- and seventeenth-century swordsmen Hidetsuna, Muneyoshi, and Munenori in the book *The Sword and the Mind*. While the onset relates to a medium or dueling range, it can also apply to an ambush scenario, just before opponents rapidly close to close quarters. It can also be the time when you first become aware you are under attack, or when you fix the opponent's location. The onset can encompass the first defensive action or a counterattack. Figure 33 illustrates an example of what is considered the normal, squared-off, one-on-one aspect of the onset.

ONSET

Figure 33

THE CLOSURE

This is that moment in time when the opponent is in your face and both of you have hold of each other. This is sometimes referred to as the hand-on-hand, or grappling, phase. It can consist of such actions as pinning, passing, or pulling the opponent's weapon arm, and he on yours. A variety of levering or wrestling throws could also occur during this phase. It is a time of disruption, when your action puts the opponent on the defense. Figure 34 illustrates a closure scenario where the opponent's initial attack is checked, creating an opening for counterattack.

Figure 34

THE FOLLOW-ON

This may be a withdrawal or a continuation of the attack. This is the time for assault, when the opponent's initial attack is neutralized and the follow-on counterattack ends the fight. It can also be when you realize you are overmatched and conclude it's time to get the hell out of the area. Figure 35 shows an offensive follow-on.

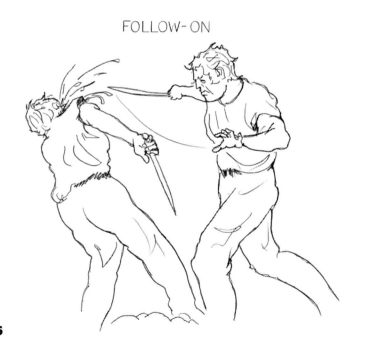

Figure 35

It is pretty clear that these engagement parts correspond to three actions that you take against your opponent: to fix, disrupt, and assault. We will discuss the associated cutting and thrusting aspects of each throughout this manual.

Now, don't get too concerned with the precise technical aspects of these actions. Rather, think of them as generic concepts that form the context for "seeing" the fight. This is probably a good time to go

Tactical Elements and Rhythm of the Fight

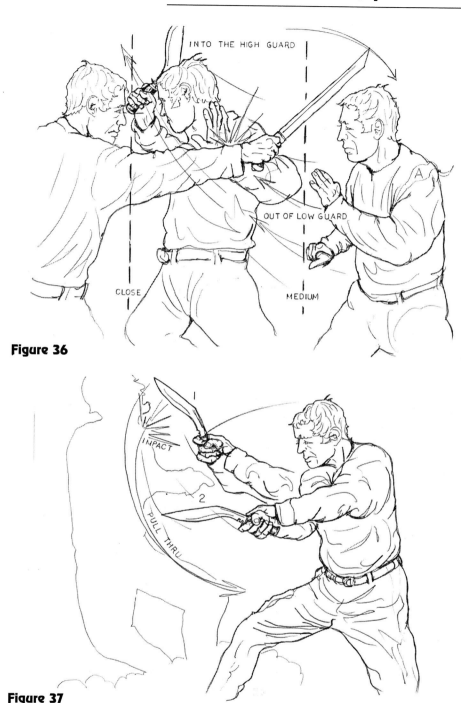

Figure 36

Figure 37

See the difference? Notice how the rhythm of the actual fight is different from the sport-like aspect of the tournament? Note how the sport sparring tends to have pauses where the opponents basically withdraw to observe the results of their strike. Notice how the actual fight or assault does not have these pauses and how the action continues until someone goes down. Think about this.

THE RHYTHM OR FLOW OF THE FIGHT

The movement through the onset, closure, and follow-on of an engagement has a distinct rhythm of motion that combines all the aspects of technique associated with cuts, thrusts, guards, blocks, parries, and footwork. Figures 36 and 37 provide a visualization of how this rhythm occurs. Here the onset begins with an angle 8 cut by the opponent. Fighter A on the right has his weapon deployed in a low guard. As the strike comes in, he blocks with his left hand to move the opponent's weapon to the left. Simultaneously, fighter A executes a gathering step forward, driving his arms up into the defensive triangle of the high guard. As soon as the closure is achieved, he is in position to slide back along the same line and execute a short strike delivery of a draw cut down and across the

look at some of the video footage online that depicts actual modern-day fights. Study these and try to determine when the three phases of engagement occur. Next, look at videos of tournament sparring.

33

The Fighting Kukri

opponent's chest. Figure 37 depicts this follow-on.

Figure 38 is a visualization of the flow in this example. Notice the rhythm or motion involved with sliding forward and then rocking down and back. At medium range, the rhythm of movement can be linear, circular, spiral, or angular, depending on the weapons and what the opponent is attempting to do. The flow tends to be smooth, with expansive cuts and thrusts that usually have a dynamic follow-on action. At close quarters or hand-on-hand range, the rhythm usually consists of short, abrupt movements that involve more power than technique. Movement here consists of tight circles inside and outside the box and violent changes in elevation through the high, middle, and low-line areas. The important thing to remember is that the rhythm and flow of movement will change when the action moves from medium to close-quarter range.

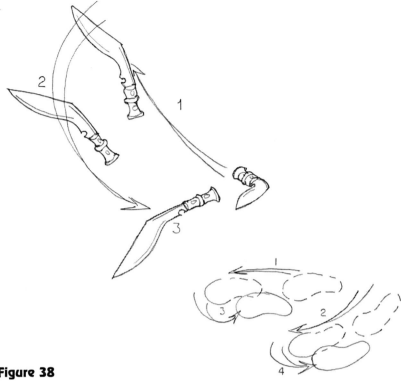

Figure 38

Over the years, I've come to the conclusion that there are two basic tenets that apply to the rhythm and flow of an engagement. First is that everything is a matter of distance, time, and position. Second, one has to read the "messages" of the opponent, weapon, environment, and mind. Let's examine these a bit further.

A MATTER OF DISTANCE, TIME, AND POSITION

The Indian subcontinent is a geographical area where ancient civilizations and cultures developed spiritual and martial disciplines whose influence can still be felt worldwide. This is an area of epic battle poems, where warriors fight from elephants, horses, chariots, and on foot. The area that would eventually become Nepal was part of the subcontinent, where methods of warrior practice were documented with set patterns for strikes and movement. This was before the time of martial sports, when the battlefield was the point of primary focus. Emphasis was placed on the

opponent's physical ability, his weapons, and the environment in which one would be fighting.

Although there are few readily apparent links to support this, it is a common belief that the fighting methods for the kukri may have drawn influence from this region. The following quote from the *Mahabharata* describing the mace fight between Shalya and Bhima gives some idea of the style and intensity of combat of that time:

These two lions among men, no difference could be noticed between them in respect of their careering in circles or their wielding the mace . . . in that encounter between those two combatants then, Vrikodara and the ruler of the Madras, roaring like bulls, careering in circles, frequently jumping up in the air . . . Having ceased for a moment, those two warriors of great energy once more began with uplifted maces, to career in closer circles. Once more the clash took place between those two warriors of superhuman feats, each having advanced towards the other by eight steps, and each assailing the other with his uplifted iron club. Then wishing to get at each other they once more careered in circles.

Mahabharata, c. 400 BCE

Depending on one's interpretation of the term "career," the above nineteenth-century translation seems to be describing a form of circular or spiraling movement accompanied by a flourishing of weapons and rapid closing from medium to close-quarter ranges. Hindu religious literature also discusses the movement or rhythm of the fight being a form of a "whirling dance" that included jumping, turning left and right, and zigzag closing movements. Today you will see similar approaches in the Sikh martial art of gatka, banshay of Burma, and pencak silat of Indonesia. At any rate, those are the connections that I've seen.

Over the past years, I've been honored to train with Maestros Jeanette and Ramon Martinez in the Spanish system of fencing called *La Verdadera Destreza*. Later, Armas Blancas Sevillanas James Loriega taught me a nineteenth-century knife fighting tactic called the *corrida*. Both of these historical systems place emphasis on the circle as a training aid. After studying some of the fighting methods of the Indian subcontinent, I began to see the same movement patterns, where the footwork supported a variety of circular approaches that spiraled inward toward the opponent. The biggest difference between the East Asian and Spanish versions was that the focus of the former seemed to be on a smaller, tighter circular pattern that fell within the close-quarter area. This is particularly evident in some of the dance-like forms performed by modern-day Sikhs in their weapons training.

Over the past decade I've written five manuals where the use of the "Spanish Circle" was included in the curriculum. After studying the martial arts of the Indian subcontinent, I decided to incorporate some of the concepts I learned into a new version of the circle that might support the tactics of the kukri.

During the last seven years that my School of Two Swords operated, I used a modified version of Girard Thibault's seventeenth-century circular training aid to teach new students the concepts of dis-

tance, time, and position for knife, sword, tomahawk, and staff. This was laid out full size on the floor of the training hall, where it functioned as a vehicle to reinforce training tasks related to movement against an opponent. I used it extensively with the student during sparring to point out mistakes and successes in positioning. When used in conjunction with the wall chart in Figure 13, I found this approach very efficient for imprinting the rhythm and dynamics of both medium and close-quarter engagement.

In this text, I have modified this approach to create a simplified circle that takes into account what I had learned from the fighting methods of India. Figure 39 illustrates our circle, which I call the "Circle of the Mind." Remember that this is a training aid for grasping the concepts of distance, time, and position, not a system within itself. If you are not comfortable with this, use whatever martial system you want.

ASPECTS OF THE CIRCLE AS A TRAINING AID

Let's now look at the components of the Circle of the Mind and relate it to distance, time, and position. Take a look at Figure 39, where we identify the various parts of our circle. Basically, the diagram is composed of two concentric circles. The outer one represents the medium range and the inner the close-quarter range. The opponent is visualized as being in the center of the circle and the student in the fighting position. The line from the fighting position through the opponent location and ending with the arrowhead represents the straight-line distance of either attack or defense. This line should be identified as the centerline. There is a hash mark on this line that is approximately a half to one step inside the circle. When you reach the hash mark, you are considered to be in range of your opponent's weapon. In other words, you can hit him and *he can hit you.*

Figure 40 visualizes this concept where both opponents, with minimal movement, can launch an attack. If the trainee executes a passing step forward, he will have effectively closed on the opponent at close range. The time factor is represented by the amount of time it would take the trainee to move along the centerline to

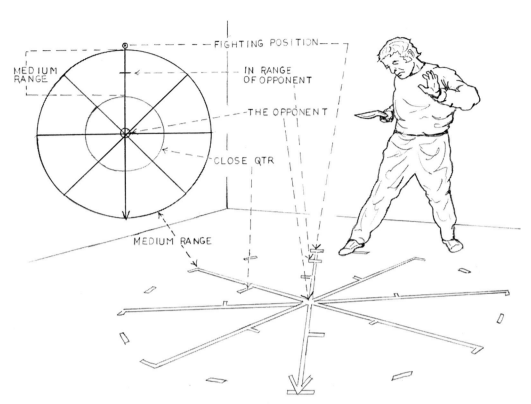

Figure 39

Figure 40

a position to strike a specific target. The concept of position is illustrated by the various lines that bisect the outer and inner circles. Basically, they are a guide to various generic angles to the centerline. If the trainee, during an attack, steps either left or right of the centerline, he is using the concept of position. You will see more examples of this in the engagement scenarios of this text.

Figure 41

Creating the Circular Training Aid

Now, I am going to run through the steps I used to create my training circle on the training hall floor. You can make this a permanent diagram with paint, or use masking tape if you don't want to mark the floor surface. If you train outdoors, flour or chalk is a good substance to make a temporary circle. For our example, we will use masking tape.

Begin by establishing the inner circle. Tape a small cross in the center of the area, as depicted in drawing 1 of Figure 41. To determine the circumference of the inner circle, use the kukri you will be working with. Lay the kukri handle at the center of the cross and place a piece of tape approximately 1 inch from the point, as seen in drawing 2. Now rotate the kukri around in an arc and tape the floor every 12 inches, as depicted in drawing 3. The completed circle will accommodate the arc of a short strike, as illustrated in drawing 4. This completes the close-quarter inner circle.

Next we add the medium-range circle. To draw this arc, mark a long stick at navel height, as shown in drawing 1 of Figure 42. Place the mark at the center of the cross, as depicted in drawing 2, and use the stick as a guide for taping the outer arc to indicate the medium-range circle. Using Figure 39 as a guide, lay out the angle lines approximately every 24 inches until it is reasonably close to the drawing. Depending on the direction you plan to move, designate one of these lines as the centerline and mark it with an arrow at one end. Stand at the end of the centerline, take a half to one step into the medium-range circle, and tape this point with the in-range hash mark.

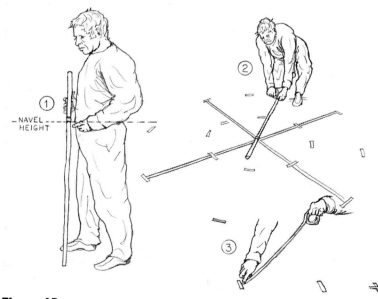

Figure 42

Now let's look at how the circle can be used to imprint the concepts of distance, time, and position for specific techniques.

Using the Circle

The circle on the training hall floor serves as a visual structure to the learning experience by providing a geometric memory aid for both student and instructor. It serves as a visual "language" that can be referred to when making teaching points related to movement and position. I found this to be a good tool to judge if the new student had captured the technique demonstrated. You might say that it adds depth to the instruction during solo training, as visualized in Figure 43. Cutting and thrusting training can be enhanced by placing a heavy or silhouette bag at the opponent location in the center of the circle, as visualized in Figure 44. During the initial stages of partner training involving drills and scenarios, the circle provides that ready reference to the changes of distance and position needed to acquire a target opening or defend against an attack. Figure 45 illustrates one option.

Figure 43

Application of the Circular Floor Diagram to an Engagement Scenario

The following section depicts how a specific engagement scenario can be used to conduct solo training on the circular floor diagram. This scenario is viewed through the eyes of subject Alpha in the associated figures and text.

Alpha is on his way back from a cross-country hike in one of our national parks. His route is over low, rolling hills covered with open pine woods. The sun is starting to set and long shadows

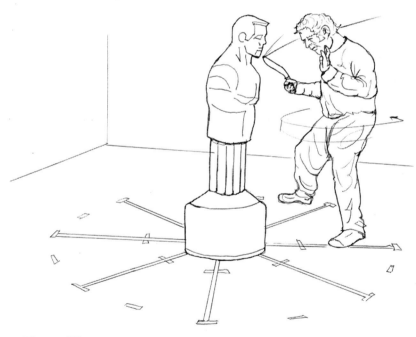

Figure 44

are being cast throughout the area. Visibility through the scattered trees ranges from 20 to 50 feet.

As Alpha begins to follow a trail down to the parking area, he detects movement ahead—a human

Figure 45

shape moving behind one of the large trees that border the path. Alpha stops and scans the path ahead. He notices the same figure dart between the trees toward him. Alpha assesses that this individual is obviously up to no good and may be getting in position to attack and rob him. Alpha scans the surrounding area to ascertain if he is faced with multiple attackers. Detecting none, he draws his kukri and advances cautiously down the trail toward the parking lot.

Alpha detects a noise to his right. As he turns in that direction, a tall young man leaps from behind the tree brandishing a large field knife. The assailant comes straight at Alpha with the weapon held directly in front. Alpha moves his kukri up to the middle guard position and slides backward to avoid the initial rush, as seen in Figure 46. This is the onset of the engagement, and Alpha's

Figure 46

The Fighting Kukri

Figure 47

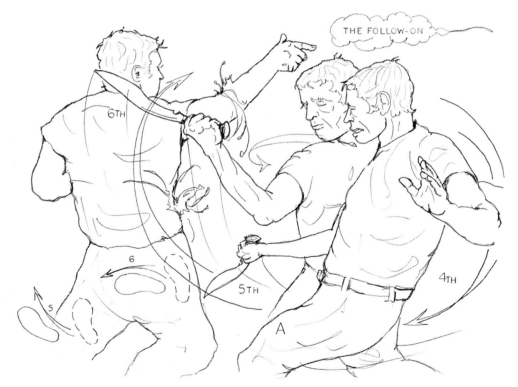

Figure 48

Tactical Elements and Rhythm of the Fight

action to change the range by sliding backward gains time to avoid the incoming strike and position himself to counterattack.

The opponent continues his assault with a straight thrust at Alpha's midsection. Alpha executes an angle right pivot while simultaneously delivering an angle 2 chop to his opponent's arm, as illustrated in Figure 47.

Before the opponent can recover, Alpha slides to close-quarter range, takes a passing step forward, and delivers an angle 3 cut up into the opponent's ribs and abdomen, as visualized in Figure 48. The opponent drops his weapon and Alpha runs down the hill to his car. As he opens his car door, he scans the area and sees no indication of the opponent following. The action encompasses both closure and follow-on.

This scenario should first be demonstrated on the circle, as seen in Figure 49. Here, particular focus is placed on a smooth transition between the first avoidance action through the series of cuts. The next step is to repeat the process with a training partner. Each

person should take a turn as attacker and defender.

This is just one of the many ways the circular floor diagram can be used. Of particular note is just how little time is passed at medium range before the closure occurs. The student must understand that the closure is not a matter of *if* it will occur but rather *when*. This is the flow of most altercations, and this should be pointed out repeatedly to the student. I'm not saying that one-on-one, squared-off engagements do not occur. I am saying that the onset of the engagement is usually only a moment; then the "duel" becomes a brawl.

Now, this does not mean that one should not teach medium-range fighting, but rather that it should depend on the training priority of the students being taught. A balanced curriculum is the key. Keep in mind that the kukri is like the tomahawk—it is a fighting weapon, not a dueling one! *It is designed to be used in conjunction with explosive movement coupled with deliberate, aggressive striking intent.* This is important—study on it!

Figure 49

The Fighting Kukri

ADDITIONAL TRAINING AIDS

Here we have explored and defined the "language" for the cuts, guards, blocks, parries, and footwork. (We will pick up the thrusts in Book Two.) We examined the tactical elements of the fight and applied them to a circular training aid to reinforce the application of distance, time, and position. Before moving on, I want to address some additional training aids that will enhance proficiency with the kukri.

There are five teaching vehicles that I've found to be effective for most solo weapon training. They are the circular floor plan, the wall chart, the silhouette/heavy bag, the pell, and the swinging bag. These work hand-in-hand with partner drill training, structured two-step sparring, and a phased train-up to full-speed sparring.

The circular floor plan works in conjunction with the wall chart. I have both displayed in my training hall, similar to the setup depicted in Figure 50. You might notice that the wall chart is connected by a dashed line to the centerline of the circle. This line

extends approximately 24 inches from the outer ring of the circle and allows one to execute cuts from the circle parameter without actually hitting the chart.

Another method for establishing an out-of-range distance is shown in Figure 51. Begin by placing the point of the weapon on the center of the wall chart and take one gathering step back. This will provide sufficient space to execute cuts without actually hitting the chart.

In my old training hall, I arranged a pulley system that allowed me to position the swinging bag over the opponent position in the center of the circle. Using this training aid, I was able to work both cuts and thrusts in combination with footwork to attack and defend against a moving target, as seen in Figure 52. (You can find some of the patterns for working with a swinging bag in Letter 9 of my book *The Fighting Tomahawk, Volume II*.) The value of the moving bag is that it gives the impression of operating against an opponent moving rapidly forward while executing incoming attacks. It does not take long to get a sense of motion and rhythm that does

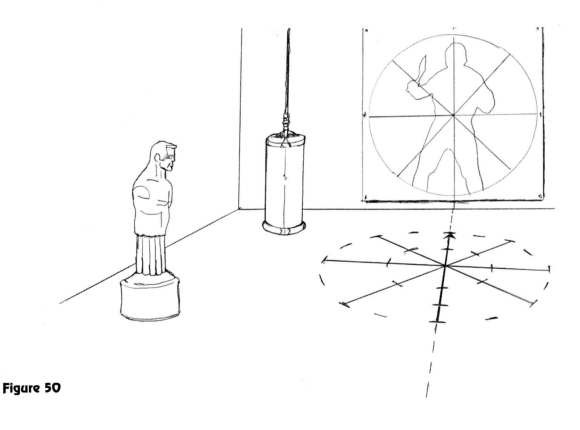

Figure 50

Figure 51

OUT OF RANGE

Figure 52

not come from working with wall charts and heavy bags.

Figures 53 and 54 illustrate the use of the silhouette bag and the pell. There is really no replacement for learning the cut/thrust while actually impacting the weapon on a target. In the case of the pell, that is one of the few training events where one actually uses a real, "live steel" blade. It is definitely worth the time spent.

Figure 53

Figure 54

BOOK 2

Training Notes, Exercises, and Supplements

Training Note 1

The Eight-Angle Cutting Drill for the Long Strike Technique

The purpose of this note is to obtain a working knowledge in delivering basic, long strike cuts from all eight angles. The following exercise is performed solo in the open air, with no contact with the target. A mirror or wall chart may be used as a guide to remember the direction of specific cutting angles. This exercise should be performed with a training knife; move to live steel only when you have mastered the techniques.

This exercise focuses on a long strike delivery of the standard cut. It is probably a good idea to review how the standard cut is delivered before starting the exercise. Figures 55 through 62 depict the execution of all eight angles that were addressed earlier. In the upper left corner of each figure, you will find a miniature of the wall chart that identifies the angle being executed. A suggested footwork pattern is included at lower left or right.

Action 1: Take up a position in front of the wall chart or mirror, measuring the out-of-range distance depicted in Figure 51. During the execution of each cutting angle, you will want to follow through with a cut from the opposite direction. For example, after delivering an angle 1, immediately follow with an angle 2. This combination should be smooth, with no pause between cuts. Each movement flows immediately into the next—historically referred to as a "flourish." The combined attacks from these angles are commonly referred to as a high-line flourish. The rationale for the flourish rests with the fact that moving the weapon into the initial launch position may well serve to cue the opponent to the first cut, meaning there's a good possibility he will block or parry it. The follow-on with the second angle will usually hit the target. Practice this a few times in front of the target until you have established a rhythm.

Action 2: Assume a high guard position in front of the wall chart and immediately execute the angle 1 and 2 flourish we just discussed, as depicted in Figures 55 and 56. Remember that this is a medium-range engagement, which means the movement of the arms and hips will be more expansive than the close-range delivery.

Figure 55

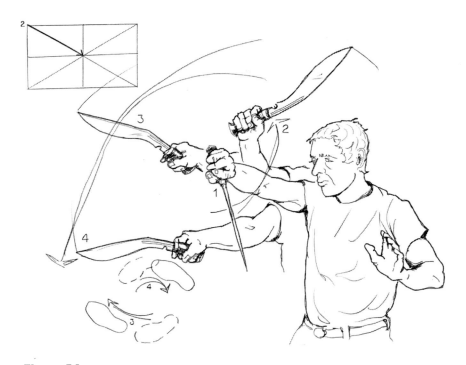

Figure 56

The Eight-Angle Cutting Drill for the Long Strike Technique

Figure 57

Action 3: As angle 2 is completed, immediately flip the kukri over to your right. As the edge turns up, drop the weapon arm down and bring it around and up into an angle 3 cut, as illustrated in Figure 57. Continue into the follow-on by circling the kukri across your body and up into an angle 4 cut, as depicted in Figure 58. This completes the low-line flourish.

Figure 58

Action 4: As angle 4 is completed, flip the kukri point over to your right and execute an angle 5 horizontal cut, as depicted in Figure 59. As the angle 5 cut is completed, flip the kukri point over to the left and immediately execute an angle 6 cut, depicted in Figure 60.

Figure 59

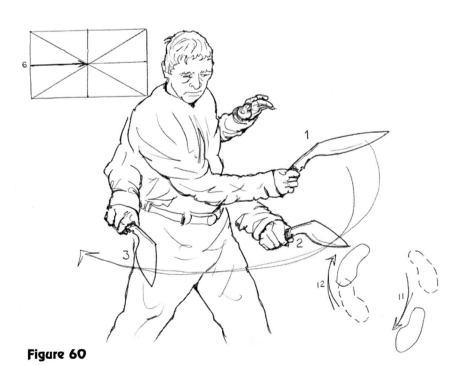

Figure 60

The Eight-Angle Cutting Drill for the Long Strike Technique

Figure 61

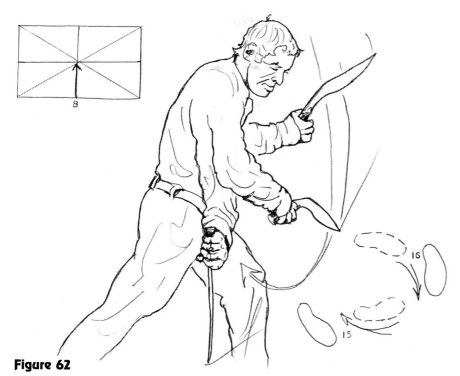

Figure 62

Action 5: When action 4 is complete, swing your arm around and across the chest with the weapon point down, as depicted in Figure 61. As the arm comes around, deliver an angle 7 cut to the opponent's head. On completion of angle 7, rotate the wrist so the kukri edge faces your left and deliver an angle 8 cut as illustrated in Figure 62.

Note: It is recommended that you repeat this cutting pattern a minimum of 10 to 15 times each training period as part of the regular warm-up routine. Remember to execute each of the flourishes in a smooth rhythm, with focus on each cut flowing into the other. This is just a base exercise. Feel free to modify and add additional movement as you see fit.

Training Note 2

Performing the Eight-Angle Cutting Drill against a Solid Target

The purpose of this note is to obtain a working knowledge in executing basic cuts using the eight angles against a training bag. The actions for this exercise are performed solo against either a heavy bag or silhouette target, as illustrated in Figure 63. Basically, the eight-angle cutting drill in Training Note 1 will be used against high, middle, and low-line targets.

To prevent damage to the target, a blunted training weapon should be used. These are usually made of wood, aluminum, or polycarbonate. Figure 64 illustrates wood and polycarbonate trainers that I've used over the years. The wood trainer was made from a single ash plank by the father of one of my students. Although it represents a short version of the Iberian *falcata*, the weight and balance resemble that of the aitihasik illustrated earlier. The polycarbonate trainer is available from friend and associate John Stanley of TAK Knife (www.takknife.com). John makes a variety of polycarbonate training swords and knives that span a wide range of designs and styles. These trainers are nationally recognized for their rugged construction and reliability. As of this writing, John is planning a training version of the *aitihasik*.

In addition to working with the cutting angles, we will also use this as an opportunity to exercise movement techniques for getting into positions outside the box. Here we will experiment with cutting while closing in and out of medium

Figure 63

and close-quarter ranges, as visualized in Figure 65.

Each action is visualized with a two-illustration set. The first includes a stepped sequence showing the cut against the target. The geometric diagram is from the user's viewpoint and indicates the angle of the cut. Since we will be capturing movement in and around the silhouette target, it is illustrated as being transparent so all the action can be seen. The second illustration is a sectional of the circular floor plan covered earlier. This captures the movement through the circles and the accompanying footwork.

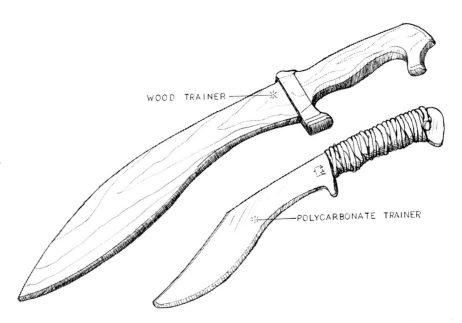

WOOD TRAINER

POLYCARBONATE TRAINER

Figure 64

MEDIUM RANGE

CLOSE QUARTER

Figure 65

Performing the Eight-Angle Cutting Drill against a Solid Target

Action 1: Take up a high guard position at medium range facing the target, similar to that shown in Figure 65. Execute an advancing step forward while simultaneously delivering an angle 1 cut, as illustrated in Figures 66 and 67. Conduct an immediate follow-on with an angle 2 while executing an angle right step, indicated in Figures 68 and 69. This completes a high-line flourish against head and throat targets.

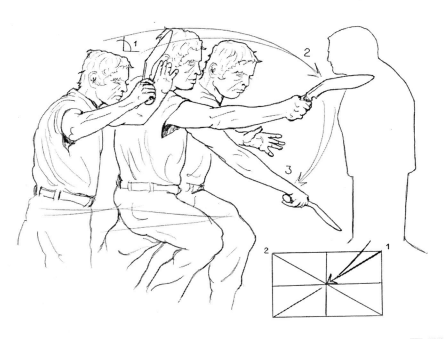

Figure 66

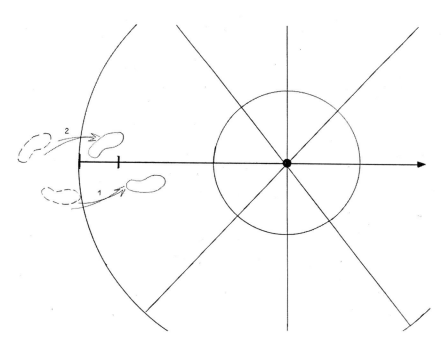

Figure 67

The Fighting Kukri

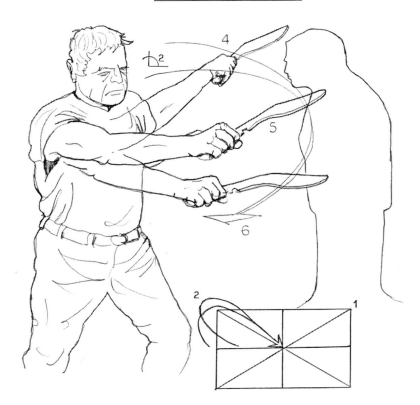

Figure 68

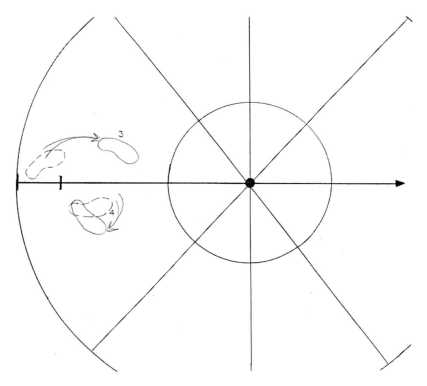

Figure 69

Performing the Eight-Angle Cutting Drill against a Solid Target

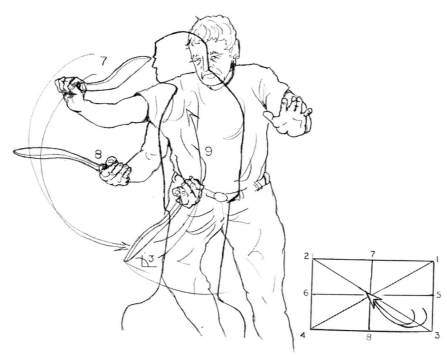

Action 2: Next we move into a low-line flourish by delivering an angle 3 and a step left, illustrated in Figures 70 and 71. Note how this movement has closed the attacker to close-quarter range *and* puts him completely outside the box. We complete this flourish with an angle 4 cut while executing a traverse back left step that takes us further into close quarters, as seen in Figures 72 and 73.

Figure 70

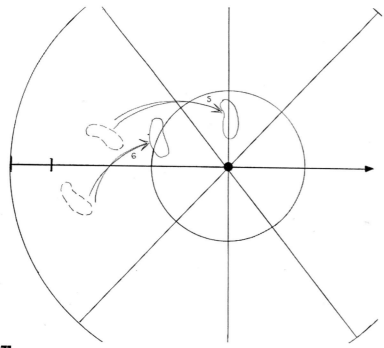

Figure 71

The Fighting Kukri

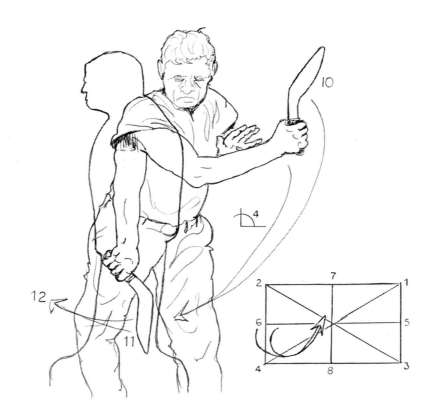

Figure 72

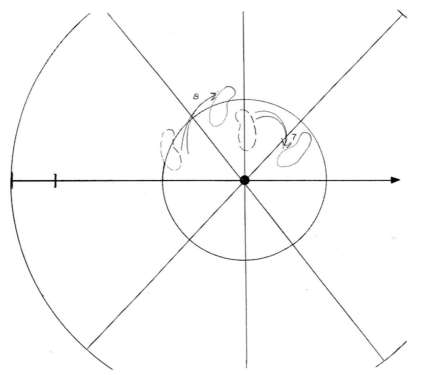

Figure 73

Performing the Eight-Angle Cutting Drill against a Solid Target

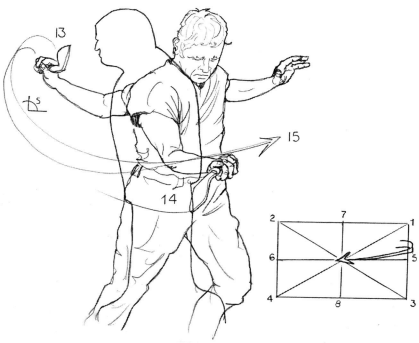

Action 3: Angles 5 and 6 compose the middle-line flourish and are delivered as illustrated in Figures 74 through 77. Simple sidesteps in the direction of the cut are used at this close range.

Figure 74

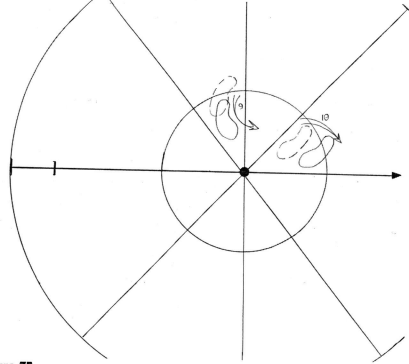

Figure 75

The Fighting Kukri

Figure 76

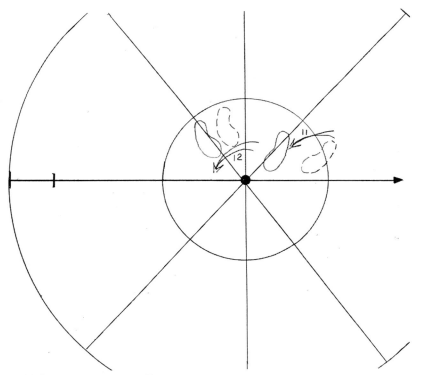

Figure 77

60

Performing the Eight-Angle Cutting Drill against a Solid Target

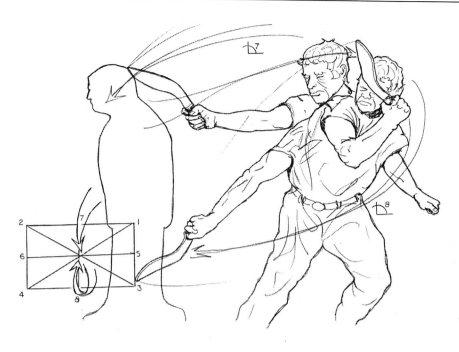

Action 4: Deliver an angle 7 cut to the back of the opponent's head while stepping back out of close quarters. As soon as this is accomplished, execute an angle 8 ascending cut to the opponent's groin as depicted in Figures 78 and 79.

Note: You may want to begin this exercise by focusing on only one flourish at a time. The point to remember is to *get in, execute the flourish,* and *get out!* As you become comfortable with the closing movement, begin to incorporate all three flourishes together in one smooth, flowing rhythm. Here we more or less reinforce the concept of the onset, closure, and follow-on. Don't let yourself get stuck on precision footwork or precise positions. Rather, let your natural gait take over to maintain balance while changing the distance.

Figure 78

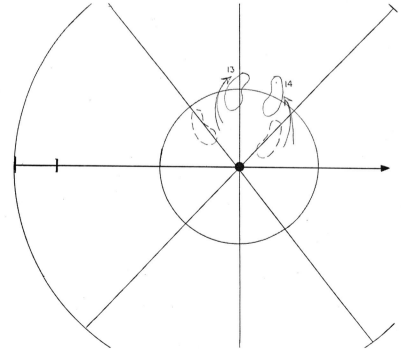

Figure 79

Ducking, Bobbing, and Weaving

Up to now, we've talked about changes in distance, time, and position as it applies to range. But there is another element: elevation. You will see this frequently in the Indian martial art of kalaripayattu and Indonesian silat. This involves changing your height to a lower position to deliver low-line attacks. For all practical purposes, this consists of ducking, bobbing, and weaving tactics to avoid attack and create target opportunities.

The figure below depicts an exercise to supplement both of the previous training notes with and without a target bag. Begin by tying a length of rope around the neck or top of the bag. Tie the other end to another fixed object at about the same height. Be sure to leave yourself plenty of room to maneuver in and around the bag. Take up a position at medium range adjacent to the rope. Execute an angle 1 cut while simultaneously dropping down and ducking under the rope. As you come up on the other side, immediately execute an angle 2 cut. Work this sequence through all eight angles until the ducking process becomes natural. As you become proficient, go deeper into a squat for delivering low-line flourishing techniques.

Training Note 3

Adding the Empty Hand Strikes to the Eight Angle Strikes

The purpose of this note is to obtain working knowledge in using the empty hand to strike in combination with the eight-angle cutting pattern. My mentor Hoch Hochheim's Scientific Fighting Congress curriculum places a lot of emphasis on combining the empty hand strikes early in both stick and knife training. This is a good point to introduce them, as we will be using them when we get into the close-quarter range. While this exercise can be performed with live steel, you need to have a bit of experience to make sure you do not cut the empty hand when it is extended. I recommend using a wooden or synthetic training kukri for the exercise until you become secure in your control.

Depending on one's core martial system, there are a variety of hand strikes to choose from. A lot of literature on the subject describes in detail how to deliver these strikes. Therefore, it is up to you to use the techniques you feel comfortable with. For now, I'm going to keep things simple and address the more common ones I've used.

The first is the vertical fist, which is common to several Chinese styles and is illustrated in Figure 80. It is normally employed in the high and middle-line areas and delivered to targets along the opponent's centerline. The reverse punch (or straight punch) is common to karate and some boxing styles and is illustrated in Figure 81. This punch is also ideal for high and middle-line targets and is usually delivered during the follow-through action after a cut. The uppercut works well following a

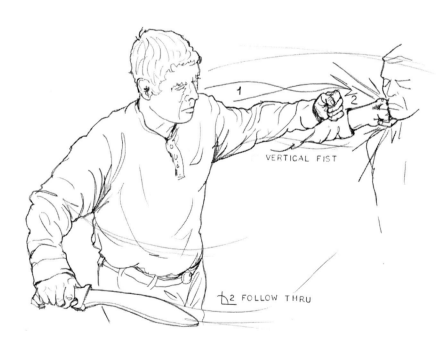

Figure 80

Figure 81

Figure 82

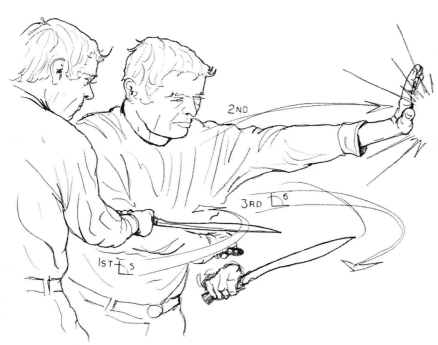

Figure 83

block or countercut and may follow the ascending lines of angles 3, 4, and 8 into the low- and middle-line areas. A generic example is shown in Figure 82. The palm strike illustrated in Figure 83 is an excellent way to disrupt an opponent's attack. In this case, it follows an angle 5 cut along the middle lines as part of a flourish. The wheel punch, often referred to as a roundhouse, is delivered in conjunction with the high-line angles 1 and 2. In Figure 84, the angle 2 cut leads and clears the path while the empty hand arcs over with a slight bend at the elbow. It is then whipped down into the opponent's jaw or shoulder.

For our exercise, all of these strikes will generally follow the centerline as depicted in Figure 85.

Figure 84

The Fighting Kukri

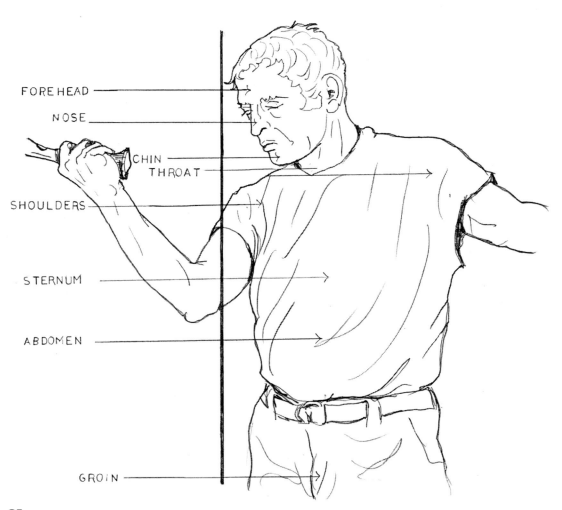

FOREHEAD
NOSE
CHIN
THROAT
SHOULDERS
STERNUM
ABDOMEN
GROIN

Figure 85

Action 1: Take up a position in front of the wall chart or mirror, measuring the out-of-range distance as depicted in Figure 51 earlier. During this exercise, you will be following the same cutting pattern as in Training Note 1. The exception will be that you may add any of the empty hand strikes after each flourish pattern at high, middle, and low-line areas.

Action 2: Take up a position in front of a target bag and repeat the cutting pattern and empty hand strikes addressed in Action 1.

Note: It is best to execute the empty hand strikes following each high, middle, and low-line flourish. Later we will follow this sequence by adding kicks and knee strikes. Remember as you go through the exercise to change the targets to understand how specific strikes are suited to specific areas. There is an old dueling rule of thumb: *Always attack the opponent with three continuous strikes.* There are more applications of empty hand strikes in the Engagement Scenarios in Book 3.

Adding the Empty Hand Strikes to the Eight Angle Strikes

Putting the Kukri into Action

"The Gurkha stopped him. The Russian drew his pistol and threatened. The Gurkha drew his kurkri and acted—a short swing from the waist up and around . . . the Russian's head rolled in the dust."

John Masters
Bugles and a Tiger, 1956

As with all big knives, the types of sheaths and carry positions for the kukri vary. There are many options available. Modern leather and synthetic sheaths, as well as a variety of carry rigs, make it a matter of personal choice as to which is best. That said, I prefer the historical, traditional design still produced today in Nepal by most kukri supply companies.

For our purposes, we are going to stick with a left-side carry position depicted in drawing A. This means that one has to reach across the body to secure the handle, as depicted in drawing B. Some prefer to use a right-side carry, where accessing is like drawing a gun. Unfortunately, the traditional sheath and the angled shape of the kukri make a single-hand draw on that side very awkward.

The two types of loops that can be used to secure the traditional kukri sheath to the belt are depicted in drawing A. At left is an eighteenth-century horizontal loop that was popular on the American frontier. What I like about this loop is that it sets the sheath at an angle to the belt, which puts the handle in position for immediate access. The only drawback is that it positions the weapon forward and slightly away from the belt, which can easily get hung up when moving through brush. This loop is good when carrying behind the back, which we will demonstrate later.

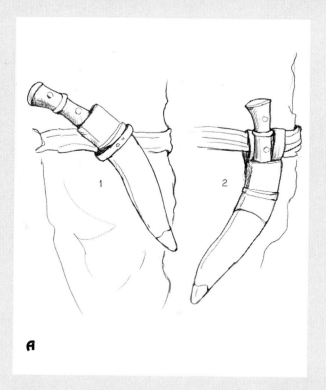

A

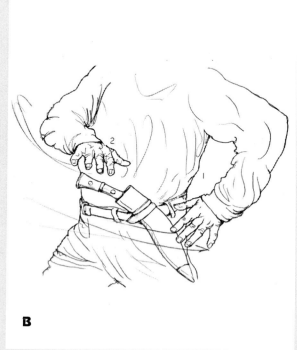

B

The vertical belt loop is illustrated in the right part of drawing A. This arrangement is very stable, secures the weapon flush with the body, and is comfortable for carrying in the field. Accessing can be slow in that you still have to tilt the sheath forward with the left hand to obtain a smooth draw. For our purposes, we will use the horizontal loop to demonstrate the draw in this text.

Let's walk through the steps in executing a draw from a left-side carry with the horizontal belt loop:

Step 1: The action begins with both arms moving simultaneously to the left side of the body. The right hand swings across and tracks just above the belt line to grip the kukri handle. The left shifts back to secure the end of the sheath, as depicted in drawing C.

Now, according to most of the manufacturers in Nepal, the traditional sheath has some safety considerations that must be addressed when executing the draw. Let's go back to drawing B. Notice how the handle rides low in the sheath, with the edge clearly resting on the bottom. Most traditional sheaths are made of a very thin, light wood that is covered with a thin layer of leather. If the weapon is pulled straight out, the edge cuts along the bottom of the sheath. If this is repeated over a period of time, the bottom of the sheath will weaken and the edge can actually cut through and into the grasping hand. The area around the lip of the sheath is particularly vulnerable to this. This is the primary reason for gripping the sheath at the far end while accessing the weapon, as seen in drawing C. (Another point is that if you are going to be drawing on a regular basis, the sheath should be inspected after each training period.)

All this said, the method of drawing the kukri without damaging the sheath requires some practice. Let's continue . . .

Step 2: As you grip the handle, press down on the top of the sheath with the thumb and lift the handle up until the upper spine touches the top and lip of the sheath, as seen in drawing C.

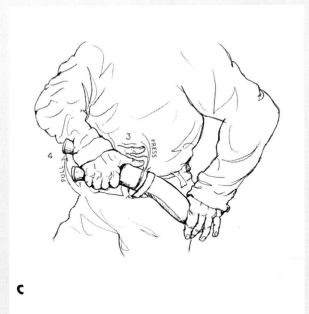

C

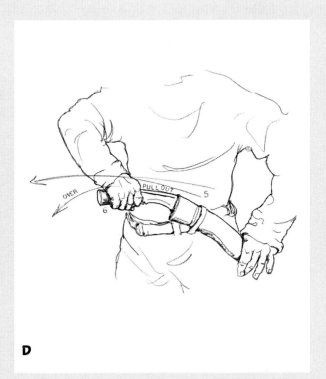

D

Adding the Empty Hand Strikes to the Eight Angle Strikes

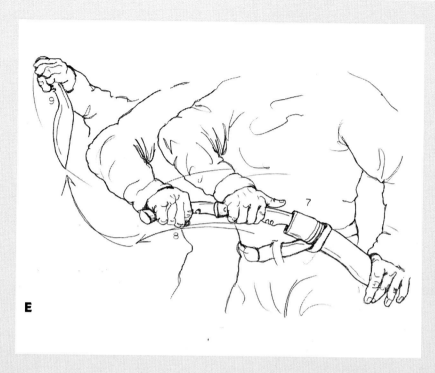

Step 3: Begin to pull the kukri out, keeping the upper spine in contact with the top of the sheath as seen in action 5 of drawing D. When you sense that the shoulder of the spine is nearing the lip, adjust the pull into the slightly downward curve shown in step 6 of drawing D. This will bring the lower spine in contact with the top of the sheath and move the cutting edge completely off the bottom.

Step 4: When the point clears the lip of the sheath, lift the handle up into either a cut or guard position, as shown in drawings E and F.

The key points for drawing the kukri are to *pull up, pull out and over*, and then *swing up* into a cut or guard. Practice this!

The Fighting Kukri

For those of you who just cannot overcome the urge to carry the kukri behind the back, I've included some drawings of this technique:

Step 1: Begin by tracking the right hand along the belt line, as illustrated in drawing G. This motion should take your right hand onto the handle, as shown in drawing H.

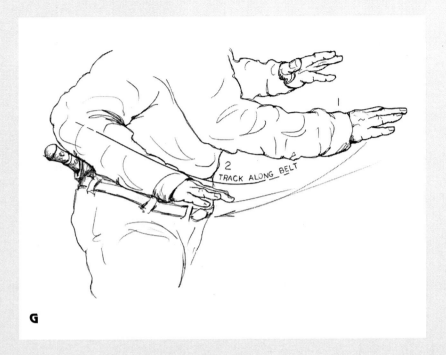

G

H

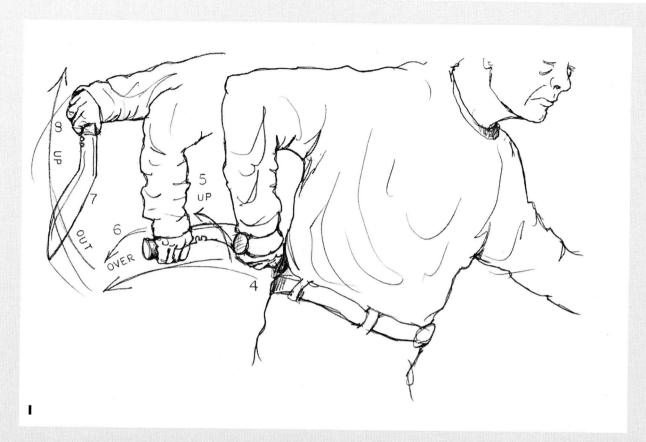

I

Step 2: Now, here is the tricky part: pull up, out, and over to your right till you feel the point clear. When this occurs, turn the blade inward and down into a basic guard, as depicted in drawing I. Make sure the point and edge will clear your right side before dropping into the guard. This will require some repetition at slow speed to get used to the weapon clearing your body. Don't be in a hurry to master this. For me, this draw is very awkward with the kukri. I found it difficult to get the edge off the bottom of the sheath. At any rate, it is here for your consideration. You decide!

Training Note 4

Understanding the Thrust

The primary function of the kukri design is to cut and chop and therefore is the focus of its use as a weapon. That said, I do not wish to diminish the importance of the thrust in kukri training. I'm not in the category of those experts who profess that the kukri is a "chopper" only and no good for thrusting. Rather, I see that thrusting with the sloping point requires a bit of training in order to become proficient.

THRUSTING WITH THE SLOPING BLADE

The point is propelled not in a straight line but in the arc of a circle more or less curved to correspond with the blade. The

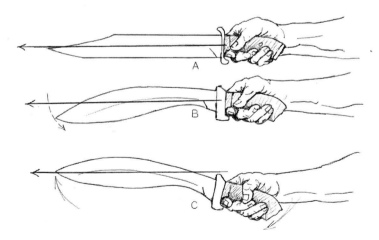

Figure 86

arm makes a cycloidal movement with the blade readily enough, but under a disadvantage. As in the cut the space traversed is longer than what is necessary to reach the object. Moreover the movement cannot well be applied to the lunge . . . in no case is it better than the straight thrust.

Richard F. Burton
The Book of the Sword, 1884

The above quote by the noted nineteenth-century adventurer and explorer was not about the kukri. Actually, Burton was talking about the curve-bladed Turkish *yataghan.* While it has a downward sloping blade, the point curves back up in a very strange way. In terms of executing a curved thrust, however, Burton pretty much nailed what has to be done with the kukri. Thrusting with the kukri is worth learning, but it probably should be down on the training priority list until one becomes proficient with the cutting aspects unique to the kukri design.

Understanding the Sloping Point

As Burton alludes to, there is really no substitute for a straight blade in terms of thrusting. You see this when you look at Figure 86. Notice that the centerline through the bowie knife aligns the handle and point in a straight line. When you "point the thumb" during a thrust with a bowie, you will usually hit most targets with ease. Notice with the kukri that when the handle is aligned with the center-line, the point drops at a deep angle. To compensate for this, the handle must be dropped below the centerline to elevate the point to hit the target, as depicted in drawing C of Figure 86. This is the adjustment that must be made when executing most straight thrusts.

The Straight Thrust

Figure 87 illustrates the delivery of the straight thrust. In our example, the action begins in a middle guard, from which the point is elevated as the blade is pushed forward and out. You might also say that the point sort of arcs into the target. On impact, the empty arm is pulled across the chest back into a chamber as the weapon arm extends. As the point penetrates the target, the wide belly of the blade makes a wide, deep, penetrating wound that is sometimes referred to as a "push-cut." The straight thrust can be delivered moving forward, as indicated by the footwork pattern in the lower right of Figure 87, or it can be executed with a rear passing step backward.

The Fingers-Down Thrust

This thrust differs from the straight thrust in that it departs from the centerline and arcs around to targets on the left side of the opponent. Instead of elevating the point as done with the straight thrust, it is moved horizontally to your left (if you are right-handed). Figure 88 illustrates the action of this thrust, while Figure 89 provides an overhead view of the action. Here the point is adjusted to acquire the target; then the weapon is pushed out and around with a

Figure 87

Figure 88

slight bend at the elbow. Figure 90 offers a close-up of the point movement. During the execution of this thrust, the left leg is swung around into an angle right step, as illustrated in the footwork pattern in the lower left of Figure 88. This thrust is a particularly effective method to counterattack after avoiding an opponent's attack.

Understanding the Thrust

Figure 89

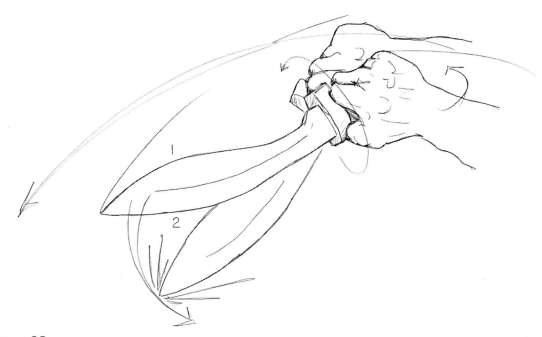

Figure 90

The Fighting Kukri

The Fingers-Up Thrust

This thrust differs from the straight thrust in that it departs from the centerline and arcs around to targets on the opponent's right side. The delivery depicted in Figure 91 begins with the weapon arm being chambered across the chest to your left (drawing 2). From there, the kukri is pushed out and around, with the point being adjusted as depicted in Figure 92. The footwork for this thrust can be either angle left or right, depending on the situation created by the opponent. Like the fingers-down thrust, this technique is effective when avoiding an incoming attack.

Figure 91

The Vertical Descending Thrust

This variation is executed the same as the previous thrust. The difference is that the torso is twisted to the left or right and the weapon is arced over and down into the top of the opponent's head.

The Vertical Ascending Thrust

This variation is the same as the previous thrust except that one steps into a frontal position inside the box while arcing the arm into an ascending thrust to the opponent's groin.

WORKING THE THRUST

Now let's develop a working knowledge for delivering straight, fingers-down, and fingers-up thrusts at targets in the high, middle, and low-line areas.

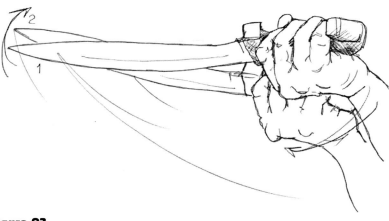

Figure 92

The actions for this exercise are performed solo in the open air, with no contact with a target, and then on a heavy bag. You will need a training weapon for use on the heavy bag. The triangular thrust patterns depicted in Figure 93 will be used as a guide for working though the high, middle, and low-line target areas. Target A of this pattern is for the straight thrust; targets B and C are for the fingers-down and fingers-up thrusts, respectively.

Figures 94 through 96 present close-up views of the three primary targets of the triangle, as well as other potential targets you may choose to engage in the course of your training. I've also included cutting angles on each figure as a frame of reference.

Understanding the Thrust

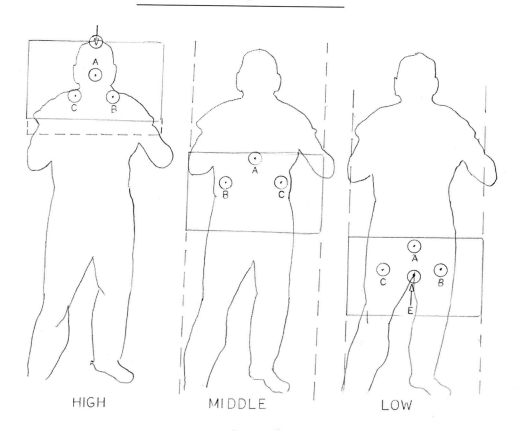

Figure 93

HIGH   MIDDLE   LOW

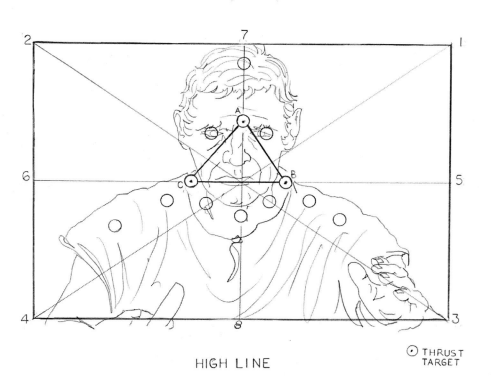

Figure 94

HIGH LINE   ⊙ THRUST TARGET

The Fighting Kukri

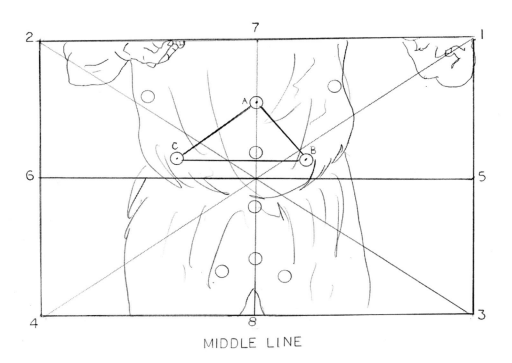

MIDDLE LINE

Figure 95

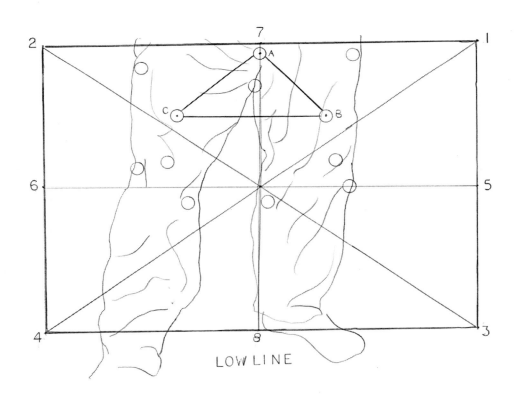

LOW LINE

Figure 96

Understanding the Thrust

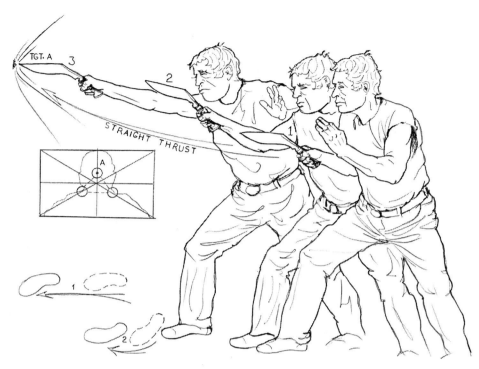

Figure 97

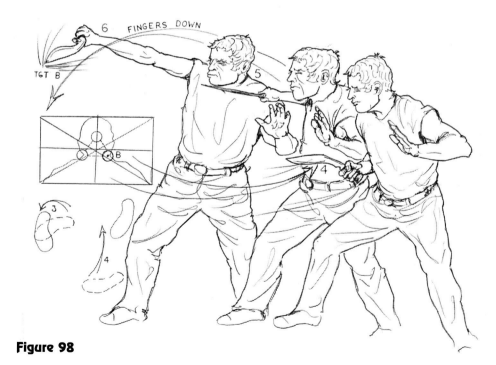

Figure 98

As with the other diagrams in this text, this is simply a training guide, to be modified as you see fit. All of the actions in this section should be performed one after another in a continuous, flowing manner. While I have only illustrated the high-line area, the thrusting triangles for the middle and low lines should be performed to make a total exercise.

Action 1: Take up a position in front of a wall chart, making sure you are out of range of the chart. Begin by executing a straight thrust at target A in the high line, as illustrated in Figure 97. Immediately chamber back into a middle guard and execute a fingers-down thrust to target B, depicted in Figure 98. On completion, chamber the weapon back across the chest and execute a fingers-up thrust, as illustrated in Figure 99. Immediately move back through a middle guard position and pass forward to deliver a palm strike to the imaginary opponent's chin, as seen in Figure 100. Pull back through a weak-side vertical thrust to target D, depicted in Figure 101.

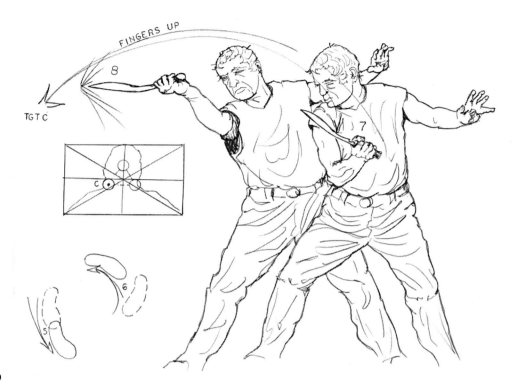

Figure 99

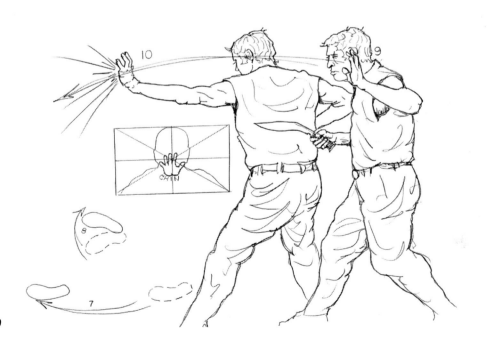

Figure 100

Understanding the Thrust

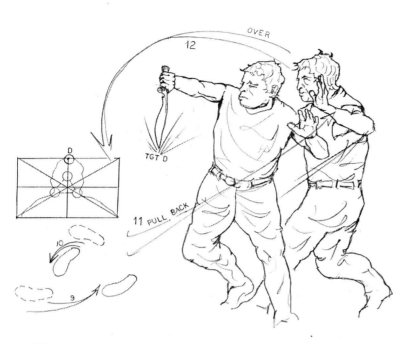

Figure 101

Action 2: Immediately following Action 1, repeat the same pattern for the middle-line target triangle depicted in Figure 93. For this action, the ascending and descending vertical thrusts are not delivered.

Action 3: On completion of Action 2, repeat the triangle thrusting pattern for the low-line area illustrated in Figure 93, making sure to close with the ascending vertical thrust at target E.

Action 4: Now repeat all the previous actions on either a heavy or silhouette bag, as depicted in Figure 102. Use the same movement patterns to get a feel for how movement outside the box impacts the thrusting techniques. Don't forget to experiment with the empty hand strikes too.

Note: Repeat these exercises 10 to 15 times as part of your regular warm-up. Don't forget to vary the footwork and targets. Begin each action at slow speed; then gradually increase to full speed as proficiency increases.

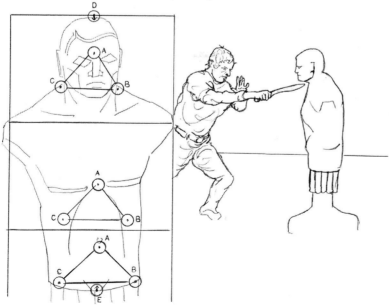

Figure 102

The Fighting Kukri

Another Application for the Kukri Thrust with a Historical Flavor

A few years back, I had the idea to do a training support package on gladiator training. During my research, I had the opportunity to study the weapons and fighting techniques of the murmillo and thraex gladiators of the Roman Imperial period. These gladiators regularly opposed each other in the arena, and their weapons and armor were designed to provide specific advantages and disadvantages to each.

The weapon that caught my attention was the thraex's curved short sword, called the *sica*. The origins of this weapon come from the ancient region of Thrace, but the design evolved considerably to meet the specialized needs of gladiatorial combat in the arenas of the Roman Empire.

The figure on the left of drawing A is from a tombstone of a thraex gladiator and illustrates the unique design of the sica. Some historians believe that the acute angle of the blade facilitated the thrust by enabling the gladiator to lever around the big shield of his opponent, not unlike that illustrated in drawing B.

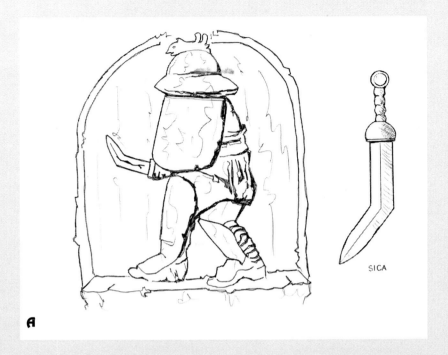

A

B

As I began my study and training with the kukri, I could not help but notice its similarity to the sica, especially when held with the edge up. Now, I am not saying that this is the ideal way to hold the kukri, but it is worth taking time to experiment with it. My training with the bowie and *navaja* exposed me to a technique for acquiring an edge-up hold on the kukri. This is depicted in drawing C. The action for this begins by moving the thumb over the heel and onto the right side of the weapon, as depicted in step 2 of the drawing. After loosening the grip on the handle, press the thumb against the right side of the blade while simultaneously lowering the weapon into the position depicted in step 3. Immediately shift the hand to the hammer grip, as depicted in step 4. This is a very subtle, quick action that one can become quite proficient in with a little practice.

The edge-up grip is very efficient for delivering fingers-up and fingers-down thrusts, as illustrated in drawings D and E. Drawing F illustrates how this grip can be used to execute deadly reverse draw cuts to the low line. When you start getting

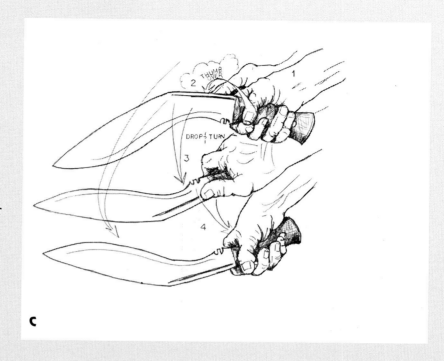

C

D

bored with the standard cutting and thrusting patterns, switch over to the edge-up grip and give it a try.

E

F

Training Note 5

Cutting Back Along the Same Line

The purpose of this note is to obtain a working knowledge in executing return cuts back along the same lines into and out of high, middle, and low-line target areas. Sometimes the opponent's action may prevent the execution of the various flourishes we discussed in Training Note 2 and one has to resort to attacking along another line. This training note will provide exercises in this technique, similar to that performed by some of the Gurkha regiments. You might want to think of these as diagonal flourishes, as they involve a cut in one direction, followed by an immediate cut back along the same angle in the opposite direction. Figure 103 illustrates the cut and return cut angles we are concerned with in this exercise.

As an example, one executes a descending angle 1 cut and, on completion, immediately cuts back with an ascending angle 4 cut. This technique is illustrated in Figure 104. All of the actions in this exercise should be executed one after another in a continuous, flowing rhythm.

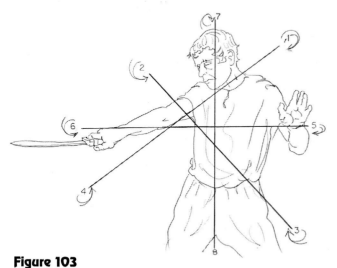

Figure 103

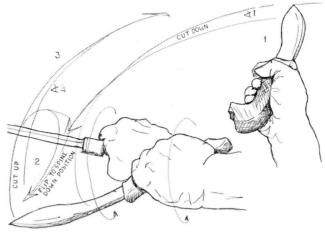

Figure 104

The Fighting Kukri

Action 1: Take up a position in front of the wall chart and begin by delivering an angle 1 cut as depicted in Figure 105. As this cut is completed, flip the kukri over to the left and execute an angle 4 cut as depicted in Figure 106. This completes the first diagonal flourish.

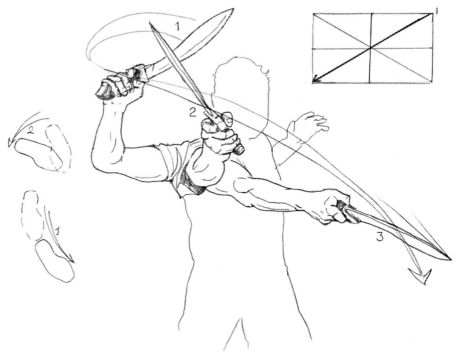

Figure 105

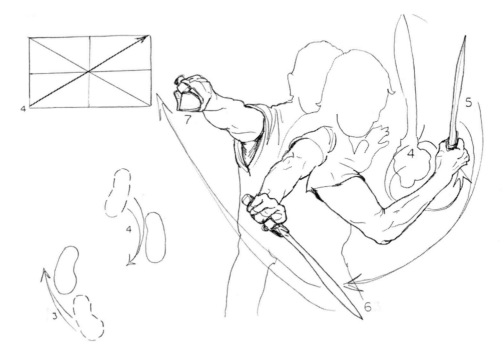

Figure 106

Cutting Back Along the Same Line

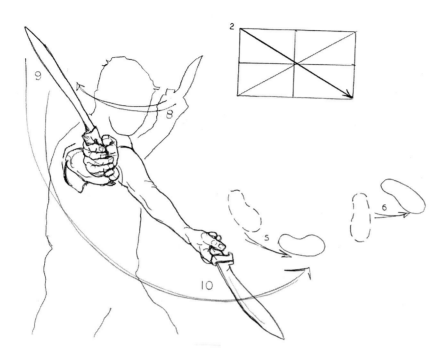

Figure 107

Action 2: As soon as angle 4 is finished, move the kukri over to the left side of your head and deliver an angle 2 cut, illustrated in Figure 107. When angle 2 is finished, flip the kukri over to your right and deliver an angle 3 cut upward, as in Figure 108. This completes the second diagonal flourish.

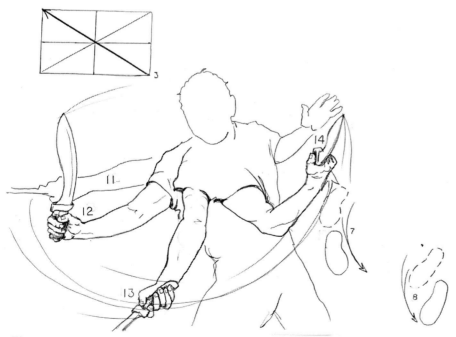

Figure 108

Action 3: On completion of angle 3, drop the kukri down to the left and deliver an angle 6 horizontal cut to the right, as seen in Figure 109. On completion, flip the kukri over to the right and immediately execute an angle 5 cut back along the same horizontal line shown in Figure 110. This completes the third flourish.

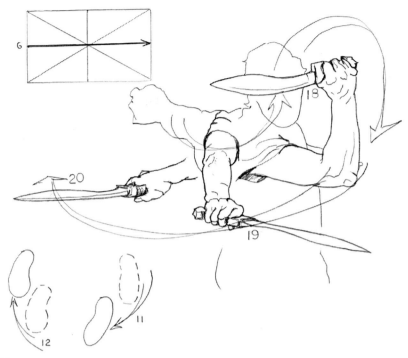

Figure 109

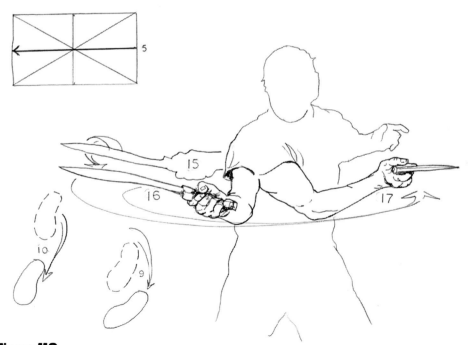

Figure 110

Cutting Back Along the Same Line

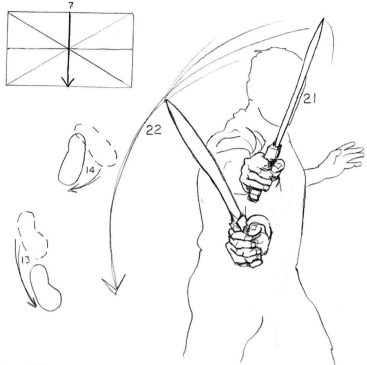

Figure 111

Action 4: As angle 5 is completed, raise the kukri in an overhead arc and bring down into an angle 7 descending cut as shown in Figure 111. As this cut is completed, immediately flip the kukri edge up and deliver an angle 8 ascending cut, shown in Figure 112. This completes the fourth flourish.

Action 5: Move over to the heavy or silhouette bag and repeat this entire cutting pattern. Remember to exercise the movement patterns that take you around the bag, as we did in Training Note 2. Feel free to insert an empty hand strike after each flourish. This is also a good time to practice accessing the kukri, so begin each exercise from draw.

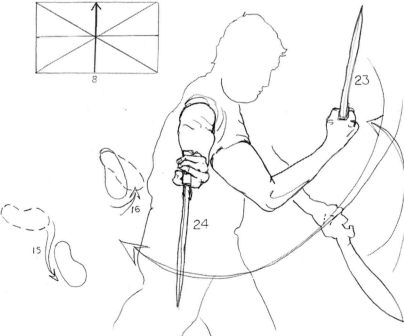

Figure 112

The Fighting Kukri

Over and Around the Head

When I was doing some research on the Iberian *falcata*, I ran across some classical Greek vases that depicted battle scenes of warriors using the *makhaira* and *kopis*. The artist of these vase paintings used a hard-line style to freeze particular key moments of various battlefield engagements. A reoccurring position in many of these works depicted the weapon arm on the left or right side of the head in preparation to deliver a cut. Drawing A depicts a drawing of some examples of this positioning.

At that time, I was not willing to make the assumption that the artist had a basic knowledge of the fighting techniques he was portraying. However, after studying Joachim Meyer's *dussack* methods, I began to see a relationship and wondered if this might be an actual technique. For lack of a better term, we will call this an around-the-head cut. Drawing B illustrates the action we will be taking, basically moving the weapon to one side of the head or the other.

One of the drawbacks to delivering any cut is that the opponent may see you moving the weapon into position to deliver it. This technique helps

A

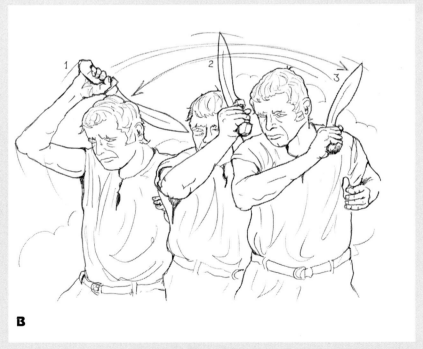

B

eliminate some of that risk. Here is how this works.

Let's assume you are in a high guard and already in a good position to launch an angle 1 cut, but the opponent's defense is not providing any opportunities for this cut. You move to the left in an attempt to get outside the box. This triggers the opponent to move to his left. He swings his arm into a cross chamber to deliver a middle-line cut.

Drawing C illustrates the action from your viewpoint (with the "floating weapon" drawing technique). As the opponent moves left, you slide closer with a half step while shifting the kukri over to your left shoulder and immediately deliver an angle 2 cut to the high-line opening to the right of the opponent's head. Drawings D and E trace the action of this technique, along with potential footwork. Drawing F illustrates another view, and drawing G shows it performed in the opposite direction. Drawing H demonstrates your viewpoint with the same technique from the middle guard as the opponent moves to his right.

Safety Note: I recall an incident at a seminar I attended awhile ago. It was before the seminar actually started, and

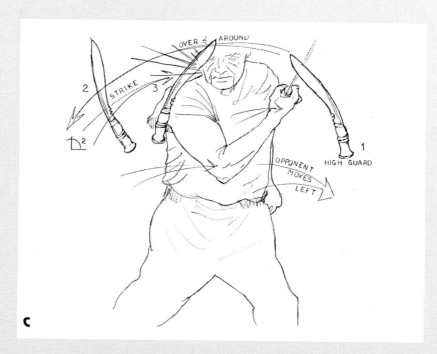

C

D

everyone was socializing and informally warming up prior to the instructor arriving. I saw a young fellow going through a series of katas and movements that took him all around the room. Frequently, he would stop and look around to see if he had impressed anyone. He had one of those monster aluminum training bowies that was really close to being a machete. What got my attention was that he was executing the around-the-head technique that we just addressed, and he was dragging the blade across his shoulders to the degree that he looked like he was scratching his back. I could not help but think that if that had been a live-steel bowie with a back edge, he would have cut the hell out of his shoulders. I guess my point is that you really don't want to execute techniques like this with knives that have a double or back edge. You can get away with it using the kukri, but there is really no reason to lay the weapon on yourself.

Note: Insert the around-the-head technique for the high-line attacks in the previous cutting angle training exercises. As you work with this, try to visualize executing against a moving opponent, not unlike that shown in drawing F. Later we will work this with a training partner.

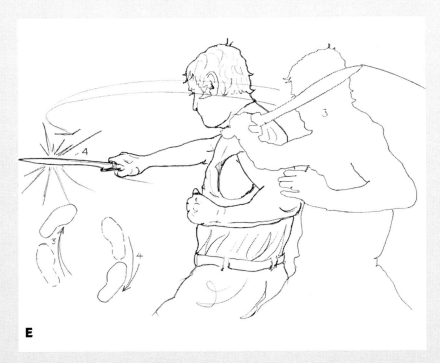

E

F

Cutting Back Along the Same Line

Training Note **6**

Blade-on-Blade Parrying

The purpose of this note is to obtain a working knowledge in blade-on-blade parrying of an incoming strike from the eight-angle cutting pattern using a point-up parry. I want to take you back to chapter 3 and finish up our exploration of blocking and parrying with some practical exercises. Again, we are still at medium range, but this will be the essential base for exploring the close-quarter aspects associated with the short strike techniques later.

As before, for this exercise you will need a kukri training knife along with the wall chart and heavy or silhouette bag we've been using all along. Prior to beginning this exercise, it might be a good idea to review chapter 3 to ensure you understand how the blocks and parries are executed. Both blocking and parrying can be accomplished either point up or point down, depending on the direction of the incoming attack. There are several variations of this that we will explore later, but for now let's focus on the parrying options depicted in Figure 113.

THE POINT-UP PARRY

Action 1: Stand out of range in front of the wall chart or mirror in whatever guard you choose, as

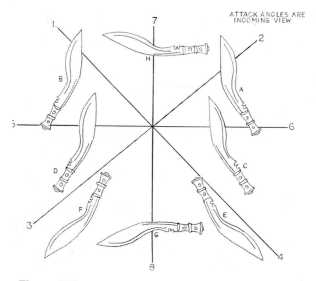

Figure 113

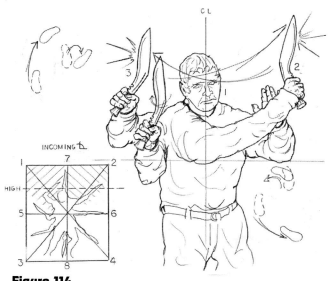

Figure 114

shown in Figure 114. Using the incoming attack diagram in the lower left of the figure as a guide, visualize your opponent delivering an angle 1 to the left side of your head. Execute angle left footwork while simultaneously delivering a high-line parry depicted in step 2 of Figure 114. Try to "see" your edge intercepting and pushing your opponent's blade off its original trajectory and out of the intended target area. As soon as the angle 1 attack is parried, visualize your opponent following on with an angle 2 cut to the right side of your neck. While executing angle right footwork, deliver a parry to the right side to deflect the incoming attack.

Action 2: Visualize an opponent executing an angle 5 to your left side. In reaction, deliver a left-side parry along the middle line, as depicted in Figure 115. On completion, visualize the opponent executing an angle 6 to your right side. In response, execute a right-side parry along the middle line, as seen in Figure 115.

Action 3: Here we deal with the low-line parry.

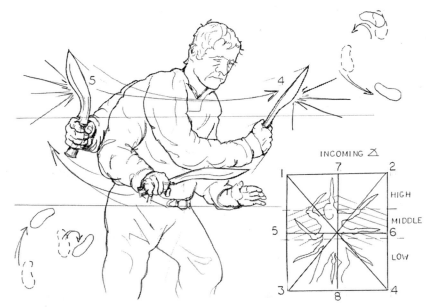

Figure 115

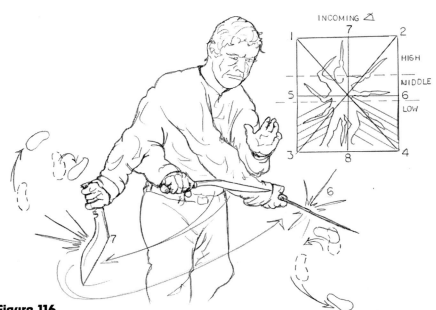

Figure 116

This is best performed with the point down to maximize the length of the blade. Visualize the opponent executing an angle 3 coming up at your left leg. React by executing a left-side parry along the low line while moving through angle right footwork, as illustrated in Figure 116. The opponent delivers an

angle 4; you counter by delivering a right-side parry to the low line.

Action 4: Repeat all the above actions as one continuous exercise, with each parry flowing in rhythm until you become comfortable with the transitions.

Blade-on-Blade Parrying

Edge vs. Flat Parrying

Quite often in some circles, you will hear "experts" argue that all parries should be accomplished with the flat of the blade. Their argument is that flat-side parries will prevent damage to the edge of the blade. Well, that is OK, but who has time to worry about adjusting the blade when someone is trying to slash you! To me, the edge is the strongest portion of the blade and better suited for this type of work. Besides, some Asian martial arts talk about "cutting into" the blade as a viable technique.

Here is another point. Hitting the relatively short blade of his incoming cut is no easy task and takes a lot of training to achieve consistent accuracy. At any rate, if you want to worry yourself with always parrying with the flat of the blade, be my guest; I just don't see the need.

An alternative to actually parrying the opponent's blade with yours is to deliver a cut to the opponent's hand, wrist, or forearm. This is called a disruption technique, which we will cover in more detail in Training Note 8. Now, I am not saying to not practice parrying in the traditional sense; just put it in a priority behind the disruption technique. Traditional parrying is useful when the opponent has a longer weapon, but for a knife-on-knife situation, it just seems a bit unrealistic. You might say that blade-on-blade parrying exercises are good for improving accuracy.

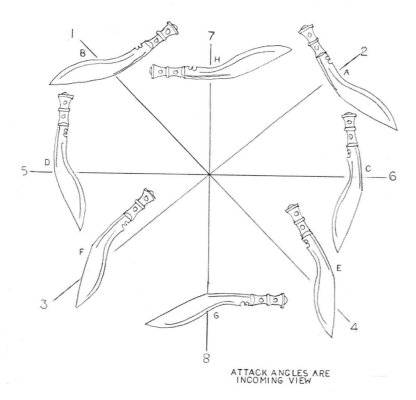

ATTACK ANGLES ARE
INCOMING VIEW

Figure 117

THE POINT-DOWN PARRY

Now that we have worked with the point-up aspects of the parry, let's examine the point-down version. Figure 117 illustrates the basic positions that the parries move through. Superimposed in the background is an incoming view of the eight-angle cut pattern.

Figure 118 depicts the point-down parry for the high-line area. In swordsmanship, you will hear this referred to as the hanging guard. This is probably one of the most difficult parries to master because of the unusual hand manipulation required when moving from the left to the right side. It is best to think of this parry as moving up and under the incoming attack, with the point dropping to the left and right. Actual contact with the opponent's blade can be made from positions 2 or 3 illustrated in Figure 118. When moving to position 2, push the arm across to the left and into the incoming attack. As the blade is displaced, an angle right step will move you to a position to attack the opponent inside the box. Note that with this parry, the movement is to your left, with the fingers pointed out.

The parry from position 3 is achieved by rotating the fingers to your left and dropping the point out and over to your right. The point is sort of hanging out in space just prior to being pushed up and into the incoming attack. As the opponent's blade is deflected, move into an angle right step, which places you in good position to deliver an around-the-head cut outside the box. This parry requires a bit of practice to get used to the feel of pushing up into the attack. I recommend you practice this repeatedly by moving back and forth rapidly between the two positions while visualizing angle 1 and 2 attacks being delivered.

Figure 118

Figure 119 illustrates the point-down parry for the middle-line area. As with the previous techniques, these should be used in conjunction with circular footwork just as the opponent's attack is deflected. This parry is very effective against attacks coming along angles 5 and 6 at your mid-

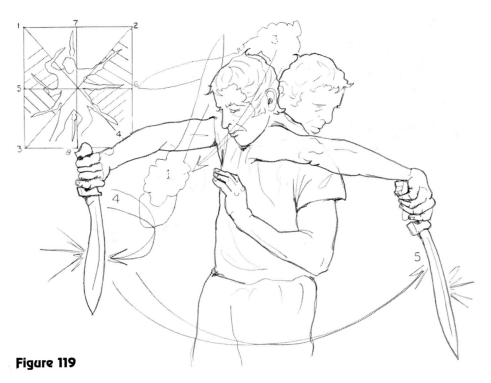

Figure 119

Blade-on-Blade Parrying

Figure 120

A Unique Solo Training Method

A while back I had the opportunity to see an interesting video application for solo training. The instructor filmed himself delivering all the attack angles for cuts and thrusts. He faced the camera and framed the field of view to be just below his knees. After downloading the sequence onto a disk, he slipped it into the player for his widescreen TV and took up a position about 4 feet from the screen. As each cut was executed, he responded with the appropriate parry and immediate counterattack. You might want to try this. It gives a new dimension to solo training and helps you recognize the attack cues that an opponent might give. Think about it!

section. All that is required for execution is to drop the point over and push the edge into the incoming strike.

The low line variation of the point-down parry is shown in Figure 120. As the point is dropped, pull the spine of the blade across and into the target using the same circular footwork discussed earlier. It is accomplished the same way on either left or right sides.

Action 5: This is as good a time as any to get a feel for the point-down parry depicted in Figure 117. As with the previous actions, we will execute a parry pattern in the open air in front of a wall chart, similar to that indicated in the lower or upper positions in Figures 118 through 120. Begin by assuming a high guard position and visualize an opponent delivering an angle 1 and 2 flourish to your head. As the angle 1 comes in, move through position 2 of Figure 118 and deliver an angle 7 cut. Visualize the opponent recovering and executing an angle 2 attack. In response, step to the outside while driving your kukri through position 3 and immediately into an angle 2 cut.

Action 6: Visualize your opponent continuing his attack with an angle 5 and 6 flourish to the middle-line area. Counter these by executing the point-down parry illustrated in Figure 119.

Action 7: As your opponent goes low with an angle 3 and 4 flourish, respond by executing the point-down parry pattern illustrated in Figure 120.

Note: It is probably a good idea to make both point-up and point-down parry patterns part of your regular warm-up to complement the cutting and thrusting angles we discussed earlier. Don't hesitate to experiment with a variety of footwork and parry combinations.

Training Note **7**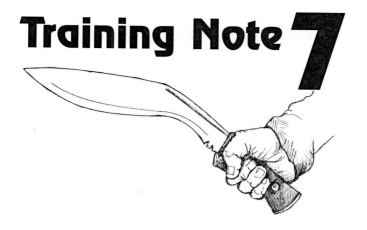

Working Blade-on-Blade Parrying

The purpose of this note is to further develop blade-on-blade parrying at an incoming strike from an opponent at medium range. Here we are going to be working with a training partner. Partner 1 is in the role of the opponent and partner 2 is the trainee. For the purposes of this exercise, the opponent will deliver the six angle attacks that the trainee will defend against.

Since this exercise will involve blade-on-blade contact with carbon fiber, wood, or aluminum trainers, the only protective equipment needed is for the eyes and groin. If either partner is a new student with limited skill level, it is a good idea to be equipped as depicted in Figure 121. For the purposes of clarity, the illustrations depicting the actions will not represent this equipment. The goal for this exercise is to practice the various blade-on-blade parries that intercept and displace six of the eight angle cutting patterns we practiced earlier. As the opponent initiates each cut, the trainee will execute the appropriate parry.

PROTECTIVE EYEWEAR

TRAINING WEAPON

ELBOW, FOREARM, & HAND PROTECTION

Figure 121

Action 1: Both partners assume fighting positions within range to strike each other on the hand of an extended arm, similar to Figure 122. The action begins with the opponent delivering a long strike angle 1 to the left side of the trainee's head. In response, the trainee executes an angle 1 point-up parry, as depicted in Figure 123. On impact, the trainee executes angle right footwork to avoid the path of the attack.

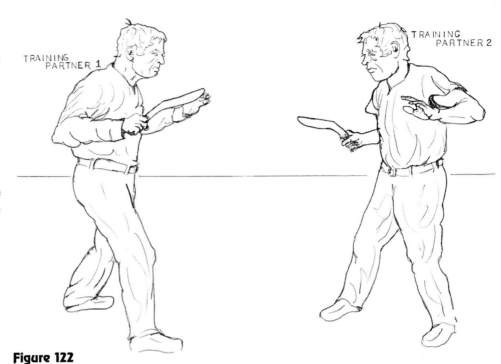

Figure 122

Figure 123

Working Blade-on-Blade Parrying

Figure 124

Action 2: The opponent executes a follow-through by moving his weapon arm over and to the left, dropping over into an angle 2 cut to the right side of the trainee's head. In response, the trainee swings his arm to his right and into an angle 2 parry, as illustrated in Figure 124. During this exchange, the trainee uses angle left footwork to avoid the path of attack.

Action 3: The opponent moves his weapon up and over into an angle 3 low-line cut, while the trainee responds by delivering an angle 3 point-down parry to intercept the incoming low-line cut, as depicted in Figure 125.

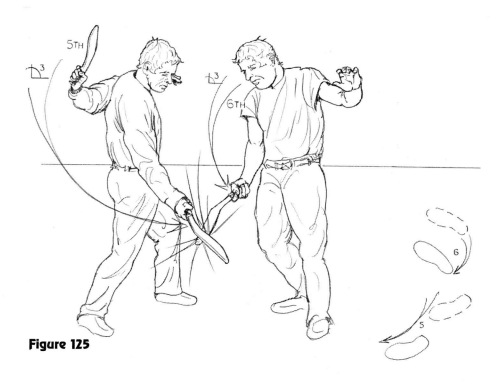

Figure 125

Action 4: The opponent recovers and moves into an angle 4 cut to the trainee's right leg. The trainee responds by delivering an angle 4 to intercept the cut, as depicted in Figure 126.

Action 5: The opponent brings his arm up and into an angle 5 cut to the trainee's midsection. The trainee executes an angle 5 horizontal parry to deflect the incoming attack, as illustrated in Figure 127. This parry may be either one-handed or supported by the opposite hand.

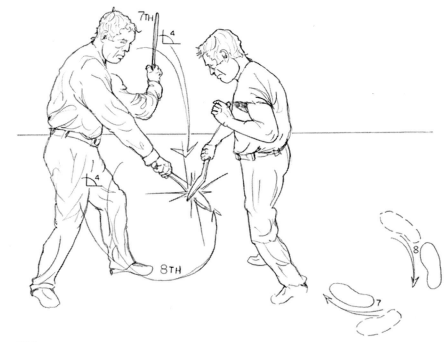

Figure 126

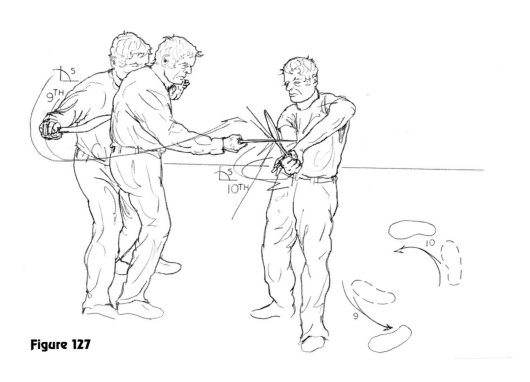

Figure 127

Figure 128

Action 6: The opponent recovers and executes an angle 6. The trainee responds by delivering an angle 6 point-up parry, as illustrated in Figure 128.

Note: This exercise should be performed progressively, moving from slow to full speed as the student's skill level increases. Each of the actions should flow smoothly from one to another. On completion of each parry, the trainee should look to the possibility of executing an immediate counterattack. Movement techniques should be experimented with to ascertain which footwork pattern works best with particular parry techniques. After completion of each exercise, the training partners should change roles.

Reality check! It is important to note that the inclusion of these medium-range training exercises is not based on the belief that an actual knife fight will involve fencing-like "parry/reposte" engagements similar to the duels of the late eighteenth and nineteenth centuries. This is just a reminder that these are included as coordination exercises to improve weapon-handling skills that may occur during the onset of any engagement.

Training Note 8

The Disruption Cut

The purpose of this note is to obtain a working knowledge in delivering disruption cuts. A disruption cut is a more realistic alternative to parrying an incoming blade. Instead of meeting the opponent's blade with yours, you deliver a cut to his weapon hand, wrist, or forearm, as depicted in Figure 129. Figure 130 breaks this down into the possible target options.

In this exercise, depicted in Figure 131, we are going to be working with a training partner similar to what was done in Training Note 7. In fact, we will actually be using the same actions of that exercise. The difference is that we will be using a padded training weapon to actually deliver disrup-

tion cuts to the opponent's hand, wrist, or forearm. The protective gear for this exercise is particularly important to prevent injuries. Figure 132 illustrates some generic minimum protection for absorbing the impact of a padded training weapon. For this exercise, the target areas addressed in Figure 130 will be used. Since both partners will be changing roles throughout the exercise, both should be equipped with the necessary equipment.

Some people think you can use some of the carbon fiber trainers as long as you are not delivering full-speed strikes. As an old safety professional, I prefer to cut down on the bruises by using a padded training weapon for all medium- and full-speed train-

Figure 129

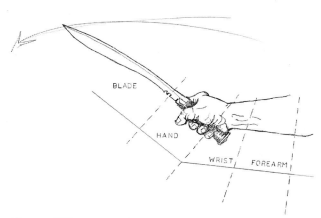

Figure 130

The Fighting Kukri

Figure 131

TRAINING
PARTNER 1
(OPPONENT)

TRAINING
PARTNER 2

1

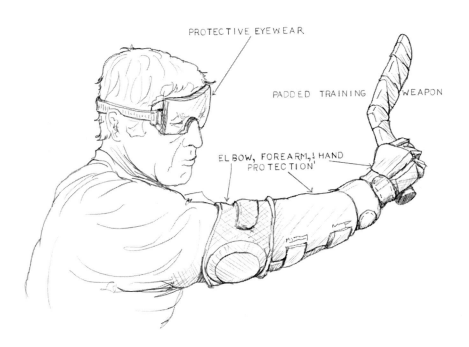

Figure 132

PROTECTIVE EYEWEAR

PADDED TRAINING WEAPON

ELBOW, FOREARM, & HAND
PROTECTION

The Disruption Cut

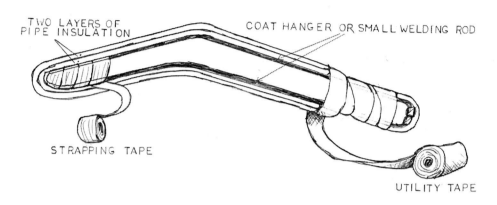

TWO LAYERS OF PIPE INSULATION

COAT HANGER OR SMALL WELDING ROD

STRAPPING TAPE

UTILITY TAPE

Figure 133

D^1

D^4

Figure 134

ing, particularly with a partner. Figure 133 illustrates the composition of one of these padded trainers. These can be made out of PVC pipe, a coat hanger, or light welding rod. Cover with a layer of nylon-reinforced strapping tape. Over this, place two layers of pipe insulation that has been cut to a width close to that of the actual blade. Over this frame, cover the entire weapon with sport or utility tape. This design provides just enough rigidity to avoid loss of the feel of an actual weapon and sufficient flexibility to prevent bad bruising. As of this writing, there are some new padded weapons on the market that may provide more realism than these crude trainers. I suggest you research these to find the one that works best for you.

Action 1: Repeat Actions 1 through 6 from Training Note 7 (Figures 123 through 128), except rather than parry the incoming blade, deliver disruption cuts to the opponent's hand, wrist, and forearm.

Action 2: Remember the technique for cutting back along the same line that we addressed in Training Note 5 and depict here in Figure 134? Well, repeat Action 1 above, only this time at the completion of each disruption cut, immediately execute a cut back along the same line. As before, you will be engaging the weapon arm and selecting a different target for each cut. For example, as your opponent executes an angle 1, target his wrist. When he follows with an angle 2, target the forearm.

Action 3: After you become comfortable with the previous cutting techniques, go ahead and experiment with the snap-cut and chop techniques.

Note: This exercise should be performed progressively, moving from slow to full speed as the student's skill level increases. Each of the actions should flow smoothly from one to another. On completion of each parry, the trainee should look to the possibility of executing an immediate counterattack. Experiment with movement techniques to ascertain which footwork pattern works best with particular parry techniques. After completion of each exercise, the training partners should change roles.

Training Note 9

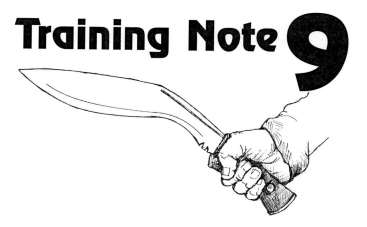

Blocking Variations

The purpose of this note is to obtain a working knowledge in executing blocks against incoming cuts along the eight angles. In this exercise, we will work with single- and two-handed blocks. The key point to remember about executing blocks is that we are stopping the incoming attack with impact.

BLOCKS AND LEVERS: THE DOORWAY TO THE CLOSE-QUARTER FIGHT

The need to block may arise in situations where space limits your ability to move, or some tactical necessity requires you to rapidly move to the closure aspect. The footwork usually involves stepping into the incoming attack and to some degree putting your weight into the action and more or less disrupting the attack by "jamming" force against force.

Figure 135 illustrates the mechanics of delivering a generic single-hand block to an incoming angle 7 cut. Take a moment to review Figures 27 and 28, paying note to the impact zone on the strong part of the kukri blade. Remember earlier when we discussed the circular training aid on the floor? Well, you might just say that when you've blocked an attack, you have

Figure 135

111

opened the doorway to close-quarter combat, as visualized in Figure 136.

When you are parrying, you are in motion within that space defined as medium range; when you block, you are on the threshold of the interior close-quarter circle. When a block is executed, there is a momentary pause when the opponent moves or you slide closer. This does not mean that the action is completely stopped but rather the opponent's blade or arms are levered out of the way to deliver close-quarter cuts and thrusts. You might say that this levering action is the follow-up. More on this later; for now let's go back to our blocking techniques.

There are three basic blocking positions for the kukri: with edge/point facing up, edge/point down, and using the upper and lower spine with both these variations. With the exception of the last position, all can be executed with one or two hands. First we will address the single-hand variations.

SINGLE-HAND BLOCKING VARIATIONS

Edge Up

We will be referring to Figure 137 to illustrate one of the more difficult blocking variations to learn. This

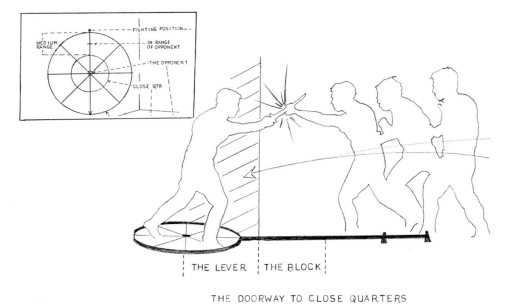

THE DOORWAY TO CLOSE QUARTERS

Figure 136

Figure 137

Blocking Variations

block involves holding the blade horizontal to the ground in an edge-up position. Drawing 1 of Figure 137 illustrates the horizontal block we used in Figure 135. This is achieved by violently driving the blade up to intercept incoming attacks along angles 1, 7, and 2. The impact is received in the middle of the recurve or lower part of the belly, as seen in the lower right of the figure. Here we are blocking with the edge! "Oh my God! It will ruin your edge!" Yes, but this is the strongest part of the blade, and the alternative to doing it with the flat will make the blade wobble and is just not worth the risk. *Block the damn strike* and forget about technical foolishness.

Drawing 2 of Figure 137 depicts moving the point to your left and pushing up into the incoming strike. Drawing 3 illustrates the same technique to the right side, where the pommel is pulled across to your right, driving the blade up into the incoming strike. Movement through these three positions is very similar to one of the levering techniques we will address later.

Action 1: Using the illustrations depicted in Figure 137 as a guide, assume a middle guard in front of a wall chart or other suitable target. We will be doing this action in the open air while focusing on

moving back and forth between each of the edge-up variations. Visualize your opponent delivering an angle 7 to your head. Immediately counter by driving up into the position in drawing 1 while simultaneously executing a step or pass forward.

Action 2: Visualize the opponent withdrawing from your block and delivering an angle 1 to the left side of your head. Immediately counter this by stepping out to the left. As you move, rotate the pommel to your left and drive up into the block position in drawing 2.

Action 3: Again visualize your opponent withdrawing from your block and delivering an angle 2 to the right side of your neck. Counter this by swinging the pommel to your right, driving up and into the block position in drawing 3.

Action 4: Repeat Actions 1 through 3 by moving rapidly back and forth between the positions illustrated in Figure 137. Shift your hips into the direction of the movement, and try to visualize potential counterattacks from the various positions.

Note: Practice these actions from 10 to 15 times to get the feel of moving in and out of the various horizontal blocks.

Point Up

Figure 138 depicts the point-up variation for the high-line area. It is executed by shifting the weapon arm left and right to address incoming horizontal cuts to the neck, head, and chest. It is important to ensure that the impact occurs on the recurve. If the impact is received on the belly, there is a tendency for the weapon to tilt and the opponent's cut to blow through the guard. The action of this block follows the same movement pattern as the edge-up variation.

Action 5: Visualize an opponent executing a series of horizontal cuts and

Figure 138

repeat the motions illustrated in Figure 138. Move rapidly back and forth between the positions, making sure to shift the hips in the direction of the movement. Try to visualize potential counterattacks from the various positions.

Point-Up Variation for the Middle-Line Area

This block sequence is exactly the same as for the high-line area. It is the same execution and movement actions to address angle 5 and 6 incoming attacks.

Action 6: Visualize an opponent executing a series of horizontal cuts to your midsection. Using Figure 139 as a guide, move rapidly back and forth between the positions, making sure to shift the hips in the direction of the movement. Try to visualize potential counterattacks from the various positions.

Point-Up Variation for the Low-Line Area

As you work with the motions depicted in Figure 140, you will probably arrive at the conclusion that this method of blocking is very awkward. It requires you to lower your profile by either stepping back or squatting down. That said, when you look at the transparent drawing of the point-down block, you can see that it covers more area

Figure 139

Figure 140

Blocking Variations

Figure 141

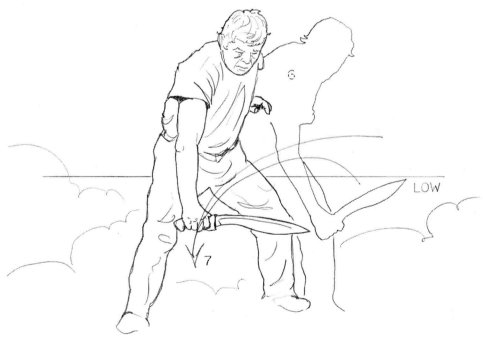

Figure 142

and is less awkward to execute. Another variation of the point-down technique involves using the spine to block in lieu of the edge. This involves pulling the blade back and forth, not unlike the motion of the back cut used with some straight blades.

Action 7: Visualize an opponent executing a series of angle 3 and 4 attacks to your legs. Using Figures 140 and 141 as a guide, move rapidly back and forth between the positions, making sure to shift the hips in the direction of the movement. Try to visualize potential counterattacks from the various positions. Experiment with a variety of footwork that takes the targeted leg out of the line of attack.

Edge-Down Variation

Figure 142 illustrates another of the low-line blocks. It can be executed with the edge down and horizontal or at a slight angle with the point elevated and positioned straight out. This one is reasonably effective handling vertical cuts like an angle 8 to the groin.

Action 8: This is a good exercise for working the edge-up and edge-down variations for the high and low lines. For this action, we will be moving from the high-line, edge-up block illustrated in drawing 1 in Figure 137 to the low-line, edge-down block depicted in Figure 142. Visualize an opponent executing an angle 7 to your head and immediately counter with the horizontal edge-up block. The opponent then slides off your block and executes an angle 8 cut to your groin, which is countered with an edge-down horizontal block on the low line. Move rapidly back and forth between the positions, making sure to move either forward or back with the incoming attack. Try to visualize potential counterattacks from the various positions. Experiment with a variety of footwork that takes you into and away from the attack.

Action 9: You will notice that the blocks illustrated in Figures 137, 139, 140, and 142 are numbered sequentially from 1 to 7. This is the sequence for you to execute all of the block variations as one training set. First begin with the high line and execute all the blocks in succession. Do this rapidly, moving from one set to another until you have completed 5 to 10 sets. As with the previous exercises, this is a good warm-up drill prior to beginning training.

TWO-HAND BLOCKING VARIATIONS

As I mentioned earlier, blocking is the threshold to the close-quarter combat window, and it is in this area where strength and leverage have a priority over finesse and technique. At this in-your-face range, one must first deal with the opponent's steel by blocking and levering with the blade, or by pinning, passing, or pulling with the empty hand.

That said, the need may well arise in close quarters to support the block with the opposite hand, as depicted in Figure 143. While there are many factors that may contribute to using this technique, the primary one rests with

one's inability to move around as we did at medium range. Others may be the weight of the opponent's weapon and his overall physical strength.

The gripping technique for the two-hand block is illustrated in drawings 1 through 4 in Figure 143. It is essentially the same for the edge-up and -down and point-up and -down variations. Basically, the empty hand is placed over the weapon hand with the lower palm resting behind the second joint of the thumb of the weapon hand. The thumb of the empty hand is extended over and behind the wrist of the weapon hand, providing a brace to prevent the wrist from moving backward on impact. The upper spine and shoulder of the kukri rest against the forearm of the empty hand, which provides additional support. It is best to think of this block as a "jam" into the incoming attack, not unlike that used in silat for the two-handed corkscrew punch. These blocks can be used at high, middle, and low-line areas in either point-up or point-down orientation. In most circumstances, blocks to your right will be point-up and those to the left will be point-down, as shown in Figure 144.

For ascending attacks through the low-line area,

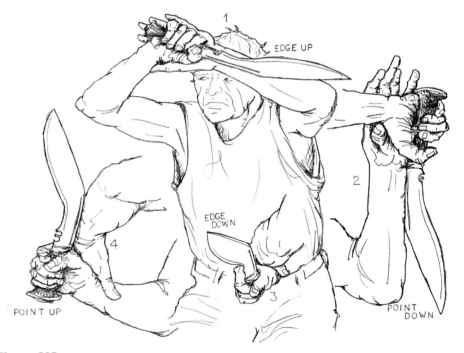

Figure 143

Blocking Variations

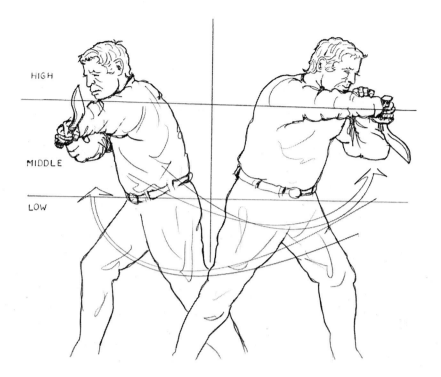

Figure 144

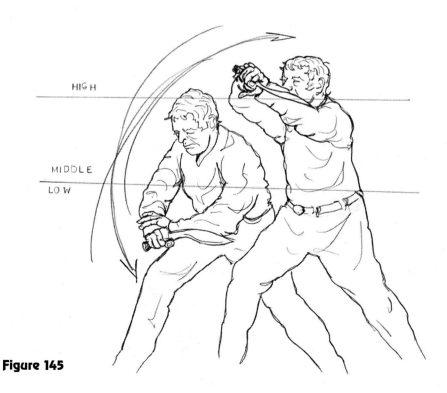

Figure 145

it may be necessary to step back or squat to effect the block. You should also be aware that the angle of the ascending cut may sometimes be out of reach if your forearm rests against the upper spine and shoulder of the kukri. In these cases, the only support available may be the hand to the wrist. Since this can really get awkward, it is recommended that either edge-up or edge-down horizontal blocks be used, as depicted in Figure 145.

Action 10: Figures 146 through 150 illustrate one possible variation for the two-handed blocks. This sequence allows you to execute all the block variations as one training set. As with the earlier exercises, we will execute this in the open air in front of a wall chart or mirror, or just against a visualization of the opponent.

Begin with the guard position of your choice. Using Figure 146 as a guide, visualize an opponent delivering an angle 7 strike to your head. Drive upward from the guard to effect the horizontal edge-up block. Remember to jam into either the opponent's weapon or hands. Visualize the opponent pulling back and delivering an angle 8 cut upward to your groin. Immediately drop down into an edge-down horizontal block.

Action 11: As Action 10 is completed, drive upward into the opponent's face. The opponent avoids your drive and delivers an angle 2 to the right side of your neck. Immediately pivot to your right and deliver a point-up, two-handed block, as seen in drawing 4 of Figure 147. Visualize the opponent pulling the weapon arm back and delivering an angle 1 cut to the left side of your head. In response, pivot to the left and perform a point-down block, as illustrated in Figure 148.

Action 12: Visualize the opponent disengaging, circling to your right, and delivering an angle 6 to your right side. Immediately counter with a point-up, two-handed block as you pivot to your right. The opponent follows on with an angle 5 to your left hip, and you counter with a point-up, two-handed block while pivoting to the left, as shown in Figure 149.

Action 13: The opponent attacks from the low line with an angle 4 to your right leg. Immediately counter with a point-down, two-handed block as shown in Figure 150. Visualize the opponent following on with an angle 3 into your left leg. Immediately counter with a point-down, two-handed block as illustrated in drawing 9 of Figure 150.

Figure 146

Figure 147

Blocking Variations

Figure 148

Figure 149

Now let's work the two-handed block with a training partner. Although we will only illustrate the two-handed application, this exercise can also be performed with the single-handed block. Both follow the format demonstrated earlier in Actions 1 through 8. Training partner 1 is in the role of the opponent and partner 2 is the trainee. For the purposes of this exercise, the opponent is the one delivering the four angle attacks that the trainee will defend against.

Since this exercise will involve blade-on-blade contact with carbon fiber, wood, or aluminum trainers, the only protective equipment will be for the eyes and groin. If either partner is a new student with limited skill level, it is a good idea to be equipped as depicted in Figure 121. For the purposes of clarity, the illustrations depicting the actions will not represent the protective equipment. The goal for this exercise is to practice the various blade-on-blade, two-handed blocks that intercept and stop incoming attacks.

Years ago, I was shown a two-hand blocking pattern that only involved four of the main blocks that we discussed earlier. The instructor called this the "Northern Cross" because the right, left, up, and down pattern formed a cross, as illustrated in Figure 151. This is the pattern we will use for this exercise.

Action 14: Both partners assume fighting positions facing each other within range to strike. The action begins with the opponent delivering an angle 5 to the left side of partner 2's midsection, as illustrated in Figure 152. In response, the trainee executes a point-up horizontal block with angle left footwork. The opponent pulls back and follows through with an angle 6 cut to the right side of partner 2, as depicted in Figure 153. Partner 2 counters by pivoting to his right and executing a point-up horizontal block.

Action 15: The opponent rolls off the block and delivers an angle 7 strike to partner 2's head. Immediately, partner 2 steps into the strike while executing a two-handed, edge-up horizontal block, as depicted in Figure 154. The opponent immediately counters by pulling back and delivering an angle 8 ascending cut to partner 2's groin. Partner 2 swings the endangered leg back and executes a horizontal, edge-down block as seen in Figure 155.

Note: This exercise should be performed progressively, moving from slow to full speed as the stu-

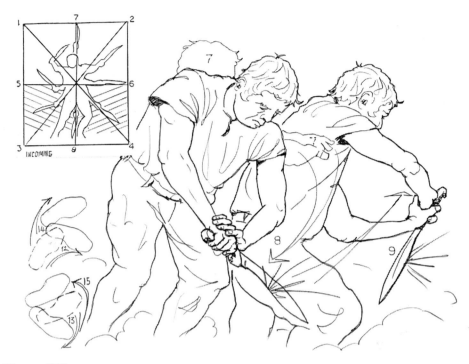

Figure 150

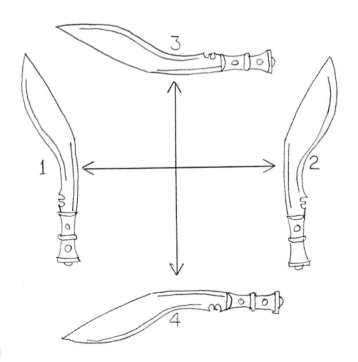

Figure 151

120

Blocking Variations

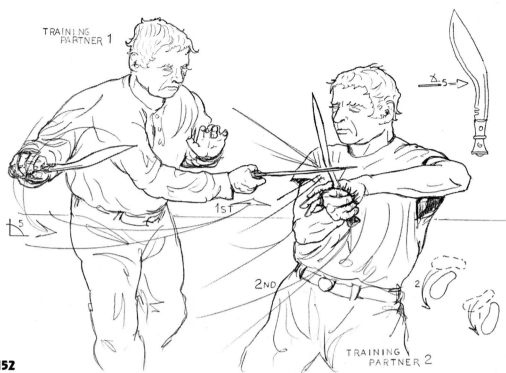

Figure 152

Figure 153

dent's skill level increases. Each of the actions should flow smoothly from one to another. On completion of each block, the trainee should look for opportunities to execute an immediate counterattack. Experiment with movement techniques to ascertain which footwork pattern works best with particular parry techniques. After completion of each exercise, the training partners should change roles. After working with the two-handed block variations, repeat the exercise using the single-handed block.

Figure 154

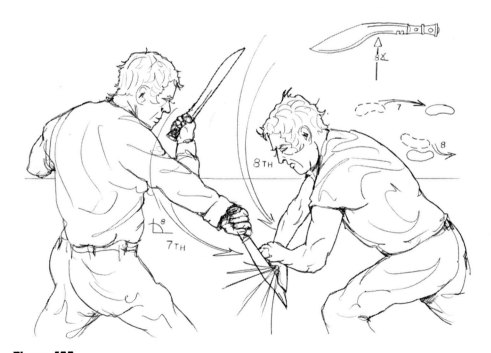

Figure 155

Blocking Variations

Aspects of Levering

As I've mentioned, when we are blocking, the action does not stop with the static block but rather continues with some sort of technique or movement that sets aside the opponent's weapon and opens the window to launch a counterattack. The term "levering" describes one of the more common actions associated with this sort of follow-on to a block. Executed as soon as the forward momentum of the attack is stopped, levering is accomplished by pivoting your blade either left or right while maintaining contact with the opponent's blade. This maneuver is best executed with blocks against attacks from the high or middle line. It requires a bit of practice with a training partner to become proficient and should not be attempted until you have a really solid background in the standard blocks. At any rate, it does not hurt to train with levering.

Drawing A illustrates the lever right performed in conjunction with a single-hand, edge-up block. The illustration shows the technique at medium range to give a clearer picture of the action; however, it can be used with the two-handed block in close quarters.

The action begins with the opponent delivering an angle 7 cut to the top of the head. Partner 2 executes a single-hand, edge-up block. On impact, partner 2 pushes the opponent's blade to the left while simultaneously dropping his point and rotating his blade to the right, which places his weapon inside the box. From this position, he immediately launches into an angle 7 cut down into the opponent's head or neck.

Drawing B shows a close-up view of this common lever. Note the position of the recurve against the opponent's blade. From this position, partner 2 continues to pivot and push around to a place where his blade delivered against attacks to the middle line.

A

123

The Fighting Kukri

Drawings C and D capture the actions for a lever left. The action begins with the opponent delivering his attack. Partner 2 immediately counters with a single-hand, point-up block to his left, as shown in drawing C. On impact, partner 2 rotates the pommel under, around, and up on the opponent's blade. As his blade reaches the outside, he passes and pivots to a position that places him outside the box and delivers a cut to the right side of the opponent's head, as shown in drawing D. Drawing E provides a detail of the pivoting action around the opponent's blade. It is important that this be accomplished while pushing up and back into the opponent.

Reality check! It is important to note that during the execution of these levers, the opponent will not necessarily be cooperative during the pivot. He may react by chambering his arm and weapon while moving out and away. For that reason, these techniques might be better performed with the addition of a grab or pin to restrict his movement. In close quarters, this is almost a requirement in order to control the opponent's blade.

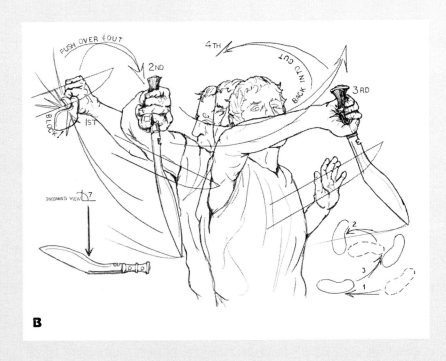

B

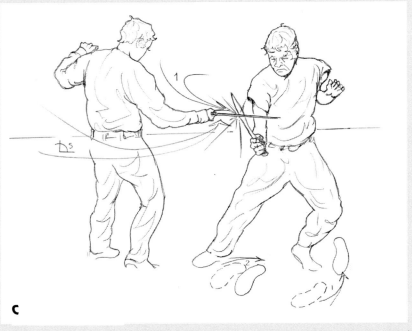

C

Blocking Variations

Note: Practice these levering actions in conjunction with one- and two-handed blocks at a variety of cutting angles on the high and middle lines. This is a good partner exercise, so ensure that both are equipped with the appropriate safety equipment. Again, progress from slow to full speed is dependent on the skill of both training partners.

D

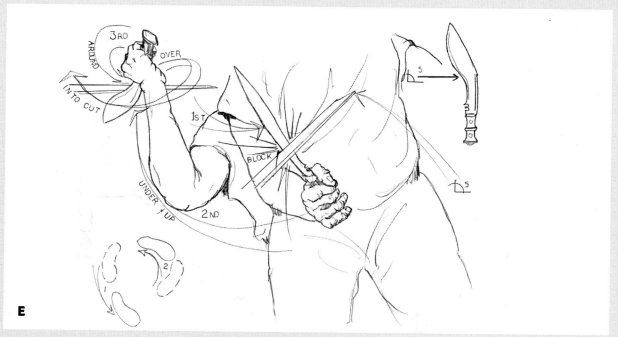

E

Training Note 10 The Close-Quarter Aspect

The purpose of this note is to obtain a working knowledge in executing short strike cuts, thrusts, and blocking variations associated with the close-quarter range. This note may be the most important part of this book—not because of being some sort of technically detailed tactical revelation but because it is an actuality. Yes, the opponent(s) will close with you! Squared-off, one-on-one engagements with a single opponent *may* occur, but the odds are that when it goes down, he will suddenly be in your face. You may not have time to prepare, and the time spent at medium range may only be a moment.

That said, the recurring theme throughout this text has been the sixteenth-century concept of the onset, closure, and follow-on stages of an engagement. In this exercise, we are going to deal with what can happen when either you or the opponent crosses that distance and begins the close-range fight illustrated in Figure 156. Here we are going to enter the world of the inner circle that we discussed in chapter 5 of Book One. We will deal with the delivery of the cuts and thrusts associated with the short strikes. The biggest difference between medium and close-quarter range is that the smooth, flowing cuts of the long strike (illustrated in Figure 157) become the tighter, abrupt movements associated with the short strike.

Figure 156

Figure 157

THE ASPECT OF THE SHORT STRIKE

In Figure 158, we see that the short strike within that close-quarter circle becomes much shorter, and often the follow-through is in a different direction, depending on how the opponent reacts. At this in-your-face distance, any cutting angle may engage multiple targets as the edge navigates across the opponent's body while dealing with his defensive actions and associated arm position. For example, a short strike may initially target the opponent's neck; however, he turns and it hits his back. This situation requires the blade to be pulled around and across the neck, then down into the shoulder area, not unlike that depicted in Figure 159.

These situations are the rule rather than the exception, and while they can be performed with a single hand, in all probability you will have to use the two-hand power-assist mode depicted in Figure 160. This is a world of pinning and pulling with this two-handed grip when executing both blocks and cuts. Generally, most cuts from right to left require a pull, while moving back along the same line may require a push, as shown in Figure 161.

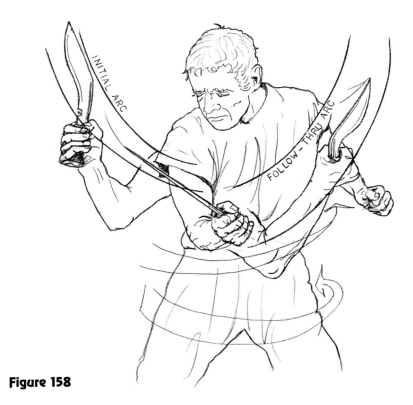

Figure 158

Figure 159

The Close-Quarter Aspect

Figure 160

Figure 161

Thrusts will almost always require a power-assisted push and occasionally a pull if descending vertically.

The unique shape of the kukri blade allows it to be pivoted and manipulated without the edge losing contact. Figure 162 illustrates some of the variable directions we will address as we progress through the training exercises and engagement scenarios. Study this figure; then take out your kukri and observe how the blade moves. Next, rest the recurve portion of the edge on a small log or dowel. Lift up on the handle while simultaneously pulling the pommel back toward your body. Notice how the belly of the blade bites into the wood. As you lift higher, it cuts even deeper. Go back to the original position on the recurve and push the handle forward, as illustrated in Figure 160. Notice how the edge cuts as it rolls backward further along the recurve.

Next, lay the flat of the blade against an upright log or pole. Pivot the edge into the pole while simultaneously pulling the kukri back toward you. Repeat the process with a push. Note how the belly of the blade sort of plows through the wood to effect a cut. Imagine this being an opponent's arm or in fact

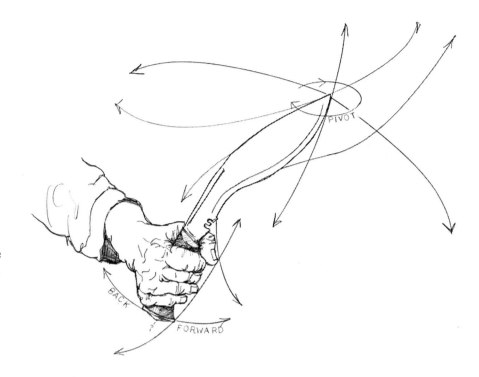

Figure 162

Figure 163

following the pattern illustrated in Figure 163.

Figure 164 provides another example where an initial cut is made and let's say blocked with the opponent's left hand. Here the blade is flipped back and over to the right and around the block, followed by pushing the handle forward, allowing the deep-cutting belly of the blade to bite. In Figure 165 we illustrate the same action, except the cut is completed and the technique is used as a follow-on around the opponent's neck. At close-quarter range, most of this vertical

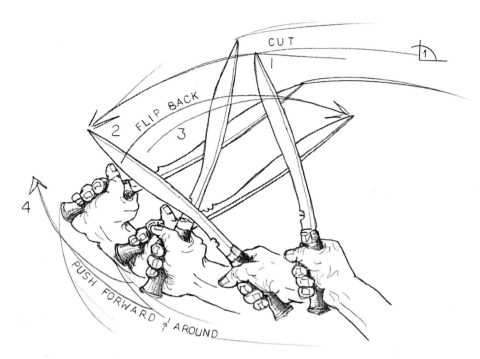

Figure 164

Figure 165

131

type of cutting manipulation can be performed by moving in and out of the full and half chamber, illustrated in Figure 166. To change direction to execute the techniques horizontally, the cross-body chamber shown in Figure 167 is most effective.

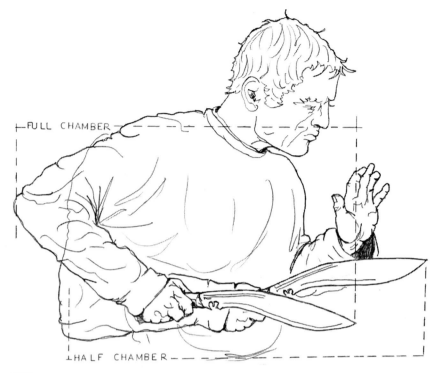

Figure 166

Figure 167

The Close-Quarter Aspect

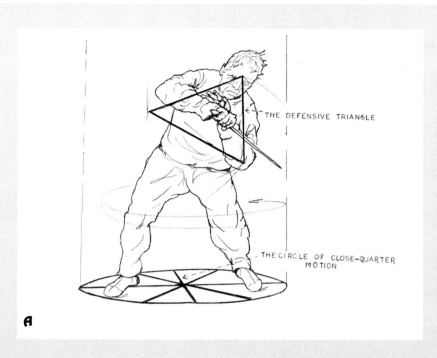

THE DEFENSIVE TRIANGLE

THE CIRCLE OF CLOSE-QUARTER MOTION

A

Aspects of the Defensive Triangle

When you are working through the high, middle, and low guards, you will find that your arms form a defensive triangle created by the hands and elbows, as depicted in drawing A. This is particularly evident when you support the weapon hand with the opposite hand in a two-handed block or power-assist position. When the hands are held apart, the defensive triangle is considered open, while from the two-handed block position it is considered closed, as shown in drawing B. Some teachers use this approach in lieu of the guards we addressed in Book One.

The defensive triangle is also an option for working within the close-quarter circle. It presents the elbow and forearm up, ready to block, or with the weapon centered and ready to deploy during the closure aspect of a fight, as visualized in drawing C. Take some time and experiment with this concept by moving from the various guards to the closed triangle position and executing the blocking sequence illustrated in drawings D and E. Focus on pivoting left and right through the high, middle, and low-line

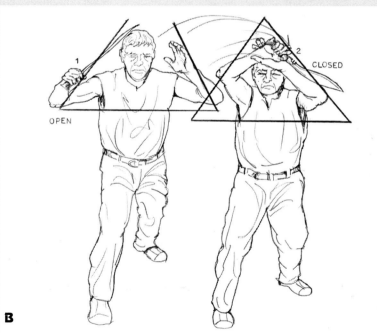

1

OPEN

CLOSED

2

B

areas using the footwork patterns addressed in chapter 1. Next, practice this action while using the closing techniques addressed in Training Note 11.

Drawings F and G provide another version of how the defensive triangle can be maintained from the high line to the low line. Begin with an open triangle (high guard) and deliver a pommel strike to an imaginary opponent to your left, as shown in drawing F. Visualize the opponent checking this strike to his head with his right hand. Immediately move to a closed triangle, turn the kukri edge out while rotating the pommel underneath the opponent's hand, and hook it onto his wrist. Follow this by passing his hand to your right and then delivering a power-assisted angle 8 cut down his face, descending down the chest and into the groin area, shown in drawing G. Note how during this entire action the triangle was maintained, with the forearms and elbows forming sort of a protective shield while you are inside the opponent's arms. Practice this as a solo exercise as part of your warm-up.

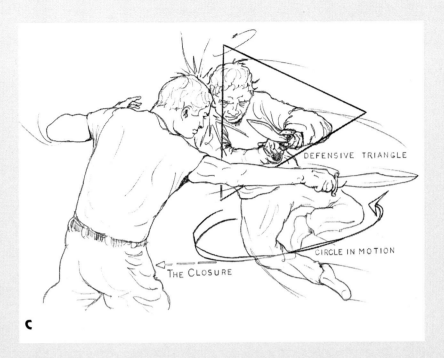

C

D

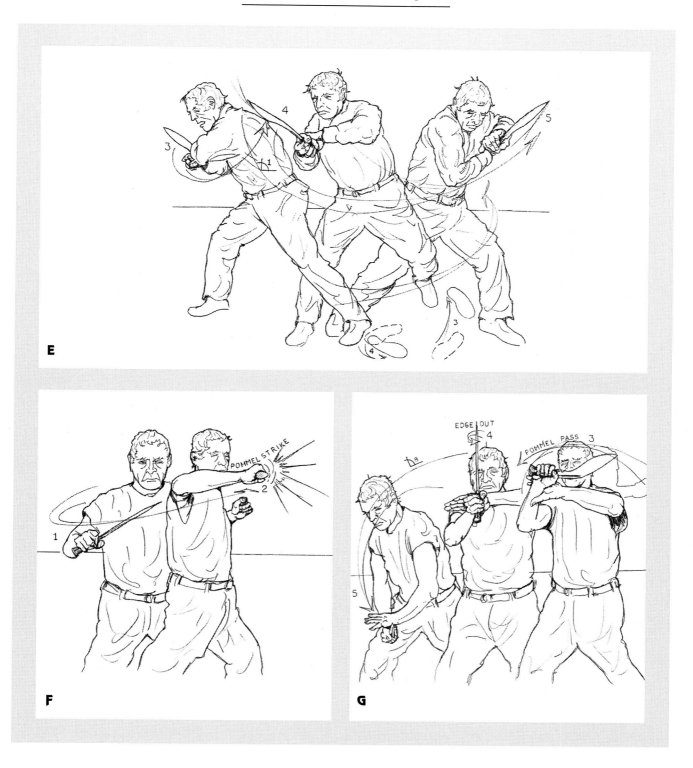

E

F

G

Figure 168

DEAL WITH THE STEEL

The first consideration when closing with an armed opponent is to control the weapon arm, or what I call "deal with the steel." You just don't madly rush in and start cutting or thrusting!

I once saw a knife sparring class with padded weapons and protective equipment that was taught by an instructor who was known for his grappling and judo. His instructional point of focus was to rapidly close no matter what, and sure enough, in all the bouts the two students closed and began to stab away at each other with wild abandon. The instructor said nothing; he was too busy looking for the takedown and seemed to be dismissing the effect that all those stabs would have on both opponents. In other words, both he and his students were doing weapons sparring with an empty hand mentality. There was very little attempt to control the weapon arm.

One of the bouts matched an individual with a wrestling background against a mixed martial arts opponent who had a little training in fencing. On each occasion, the wrestler closed and took his opponent to the ground, stabbing away but also getting stabbed in the process. This seemed impressive and immediately got the praise of the instructor. When the video was reviewed, nothing was said about the fact that the wrestler got stabbed and cut in vital areas before he even laid hands on the opponent.

Later, I saw a good example of what one should do. In this bout, one opponent executed a straight thrust; the other immediately passed his hand and drove his shoulder up and under the weapon arm, knocking the opponent off balance while executing an effective cut to the abdomen. Before the opponent could recover his balance, he was pushed to the ground and his weapon arm pinned. In this example, the weapon arm was controlled and the victor used position and balance to effect his kill.

I included this story simply as an example of one of the bad habits that can develop from free sparring when the weapon is not taken into account. In short, you *must* "deal with the steel" as visualized in Figure 168.

SEIZING, PULLING, PINNING, PASSING

There are basically four methods of using the empty hand to control an opponent's weapon arm. These are the seize or grab, the pull, the pin, and the pass. All of these can be used in conjunction with the empty hand strikes we discussed earlier.

The Seize

Here we are basically grabbing and holding the weapon arm and directing it away from our body. Usually the thumb is underneath the opponent's arm, and a slight torque is applied to help secure and/or direct movement. Figure 169 depicts a generic seizure of an opponent's blade arm.

The Pull

This is usually the follow-on action after a seizure, where the feet, knees, and hips are used to further unbalance an opponent and create a target opportunity. Figure 170 illustrates a generic pull to set up a sweep of the opponent's legs.

Figure 169

Figure 170

The Pin

This is a high-impact technique that is usually performed from outside the box after avoiding an attack. The empty hand is driven forcefully into the opponent's arm on or near the elbow joint, as depicted in Figure 171. This is accomplished with a violent, rapid closure, which may be followed by a shoulder block or knee strike to the opponent's knee.

The Pass

Basically, with a pass we are slapping an opponent's incoming thrust or cutting off the line of attack. The pass may impact on the opponent's forearm, elbow joint, or weapon hand, as shown in Figure 172.

Figure 171

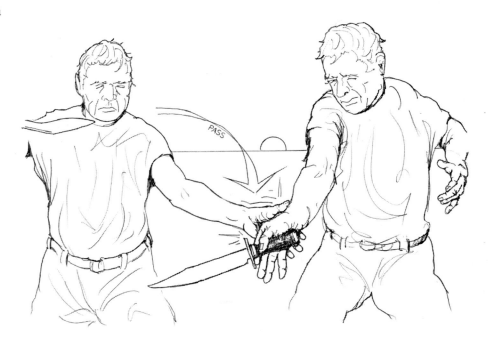

Figure 172

Training Note  11 More on Dealing with the Steel

In addition to the seize, pin, pull, and pass, there are three other elements that are effective for dealing with the steel. You might say these are disruption techniques that can distract or unbalance your opponent. I am talking about pushing, blocking, and using elbow strikes, primarily into the high-line area.

Figure 173 shows an example that represents the rapid closure and use of these techniques. Here the fighter blocks the opponent's incoming strike with an open hand to deal with the steel. He immediately drives in, violently pushing the opponent's weapon arm upward. He follows with an immediate pommel strike, then an elbow strike to unbalance the opponent. At this point, the fighter is free to effect any follow-on action he desires.

To rapidly close the distance, our fighter could use not only advancing or passing steps but a leap or charge. What's the difference? Advancing or passing steps are performed with the feet relatively flat on the ground. The leap and charge (as well as the dodge) are performed on the balls of the feet. Both feet are raised approximately 1 to 2 inches off the floor, as depicted in Figure 174. This foot positioning is used extensively in football (e.g., in the stances of interior

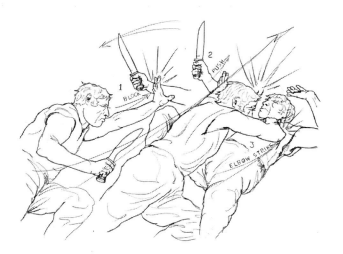

Figure 173

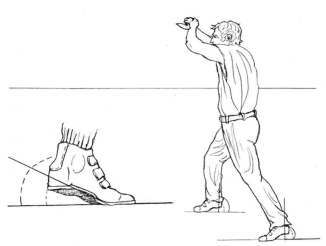

Figure 174

linemen) and the martial art of kendo. Being on the balls of the feet gives you powerful directional movement that allows you to rapidly cover a lot of ground when attacking or disengaging.

Figure 175 illustrates the action for a forward leap. Normally, the push comes from a violent extension of the trailing leg while simultaneously driving the knee of the lead leg up and out. The difference between this and the fencing lunge is that the weapon is not extended and the intent is to deal with the opponent's steel rather than attack a point target.

Figure 176 illustrates the leap back. It is executed by violently pushing off with both feet and then kicking the trailing leg back. This is normally used to disengage from an opponent and is often performed in conjunction with a descending strike.

Figure 177 illustrates the dodge, which is used to rapidly change direction or execute lateral movement off the centerline. It is performed the same to the left or right and begins by planting the lead foot and then driving the knee of the trailing leg out to the side. This is a good technique for quickly moving from inside to outside the box in conjunction with a pin or strike.

Figure 175

Figure 176

More on Dealing with the Steel

Figure 178 illustrates what I refer to as a lineman's charge. Normally, closure begins from a crouched position with the arms in a middle or high guard. As with the other techniques, this begins on the balls of the feet. The attacker explodes forward, taking short, choppy steps to move into close range. This technique works well when following a dodge or half step to either side.

Using the example illustrated in Figure 173 as a guide, take some time to experiment with these with a heavy bag as your target. Focus on closing the distance and pinning, passing, blocking, and pushing to deal with the steel.

To work pushing, blocking, and elbow striking, we will assume we have closed distance to the inner circle.

Figure 177

Figure 178

Action 1: The opponent approaches rapidly and delivers a straight thrust to the fighter's midsection. The fighter, moving too, plants his lead foot and executes an angle left step, which takes him outside the box. At the same time, he drives a palm strike to the opponent's elbow/forearm, as illustrated in Figure 179. Before the opponent can recover and pull back, the fighter deals with the steel by pinning the weapon arm while stepping around and into an elbow strike to the throat, as illustrated in Figure 180. (A pommel strike could also be delivered prior to the elbow strike in the event the opponent raises his left hand to defend. If this is successful, the elbow strike may be the follow-on by driving over and down behind the block.) Again, before the opponent can recover, the fighter cuts back along the line of the elbow strike into the opponent's throat and immediately follows with an elbow strike with the left arm, as shown in Figure 181.

Although the illustrations show this sequence as a static event, Figures 179 through 181 should be viewed as one continuous, flowing motion. The important point to remember in this close-quarter scenario is that once the action

Figure 179

Figure 180

Figure 181

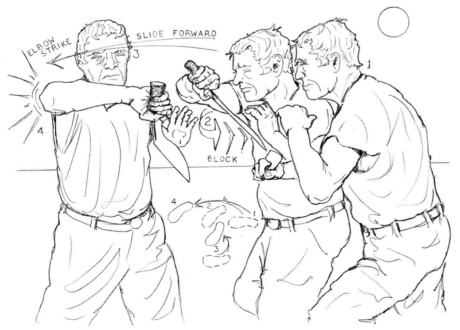

Figure 182

begins, it does not stop until the opponent goes down. Since the odds of getting cut at this range are great, there is no option to stop at any point to let the opponent recover. This does not mean to rush blindly in, cutting and stabbing, but rather to deal with the steel, then finish the action rapidly.

Note: Practice this scenario on a heavy bag to set the sequence in your mind; then begin to work with a training partner. Make sure to use training weapons and protective equipment, and take turns being the fighter and opponent. As you progress, begin to increase the speed.

Action 2: Figures 182 and 183 illustrate the flow for another set that follows the scenario we discussed in Action 1. For clarity, we will not show the opponent's actions. In this case, visualize the opponent delivering an angle 1 cut to the left side of our fighter's neck. He instinctively executes a point-down block out of a middle guard and immediately slides inside the box and delivers an elbow strike to the opponent's chin, as illustrated in Figure 182. The fighter immediately follows with an angle 2 short strike cut to the right side of the opponent's neck. He continues the movement by pivoting right and throwing a left elbow strike to the opponent's temple, as shown in Figure 183.

Action 2 provides a classic example for how blocks are the gateway to the close-quarter circle. Here the point-down block opens the door for closing to deliver a disruptive elbow strike to the opponent's face, followed by an immediate cut to the neck, followed by a second elbow strike. Once again, it is important that the action is continuous, flowing from elbow strike to cut to elbow strike. The opponent is not given a chance to recover or disengage.

Note: Practice this scenario on a heavy bag to set the sequence in your mind; then begin to work with a training partner. Make sure to use training weapons and protective equipment, and take turns being the fighter and opponent. As you progress, begin to increase the speed. This exercise is also ideal when the training partner is equipped with blocking pads on each hand, forcing the student to focus on acquiring the target rather than just hitting the stationary heavy bag.

Action 3: A variation of the previous high-line examples is illustrated in Figures 184 and 185. In this scenario, we begin by

Figure 183

Figure 184

executing a point-up block to an incoming angle 1 attack on the high line, which opens the door to an immediate elbow strike with the weapon arm, as shown in Figure 184. An angle 2 short strike cut follows to the opponent's neck, and the fighter concludes with a palm strike to the chin or chest, depicted in Figure 185. The lessons and training notes for this action are the same as the previous ones.

Figure 185

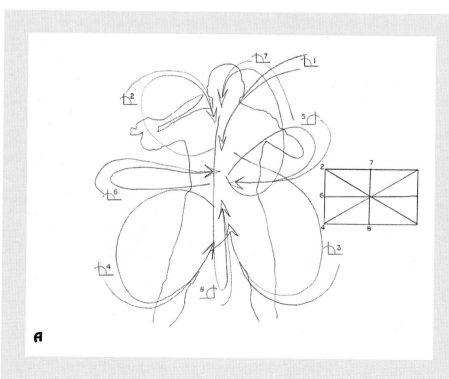

Another Approach to Cutting, Pinning, and Passing

Drawing A depicts the nineteenth-century cutting pattern that we used to illustrate the long strike cutting techniques. This pattern consisted of a series of cutting flourishes that flowed from high to low and back to middle-line target areas. This approach more or less kept the focus inside the box, although it could be used outside as well.

That said, I would like to introduce another approach, used in sixteenth-century Germany, where the flow goes down the opponent's left side and around and up his right. Drawing B illustrates the left-to-right flow of this pattern. I found this pattern to be particularly efficient delivering the cuts while moving outside the box, as conceptualized in drawing C.

During this exercise, you can insert palm strikes, pins, and passes, alternating with the series of short strike cuts. Pay particular attention to the footwork patterns that take you around the target area. This exercise should be practiced solo in front of a wall chart or mirror; then progress to executing it on a heavy bag.

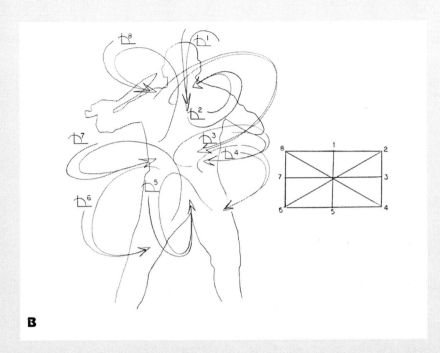

B

C

More on Dealing with the Steel

Action 1: Begin by visualizing an incoming angle 1 to the left side of your head. Slide forward and execute a point-down block and immediately follow by seizing the opponent's weapon wrist, as conceptualized in drawing D. Pull the opponent's arm out and to your left and follow with an angle 1 chop to the top of his head, as shown in drawing E. These sequences are executed while moving in a circular pattern similar to angle right stepping.

D

E

Action 2: Continue to turn in a circular manner to your right around the opponent. Execute a point-down parry against an incoming angle 5 to your midsection. Lift the weapon arm up and around while reaching forward with the left hand to execute a pin or palm strike, as depicted in drawing F. As illustrated in drawing G, swing the kukri around the head and into an angle 2 cut to your opponent's neck.

F

G

More on Dealing with the Steel

H

Action 3: Visualize the opponent delivering another angle 5 at your midsection and counter by turning away from the cut and executing another point-down parry, as depicted in drawing H. While continuing the turn to the outside, reach out and grab the opponent's arm; immediately pull back and deliver an angle 3 cut to his midsection as in drawing I.

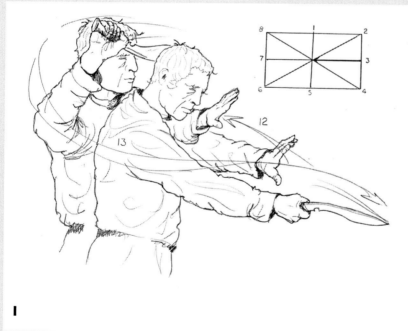

I

Action 4: Continuing to turn to the right, raise the kukri up and to the right and execute a point-up parry to counter an incoming angle 2 attack. Continue the flow through the parry into an angle 4 attack up into the opponent's groin, as illustrated in drawing J. During the follow-through from the cut, continue to raise the kukri up through an edge-up, point-right block as shown in drawing K. Immediately follow with an angle 5 cut over, down, and up into the opponent's groin area.

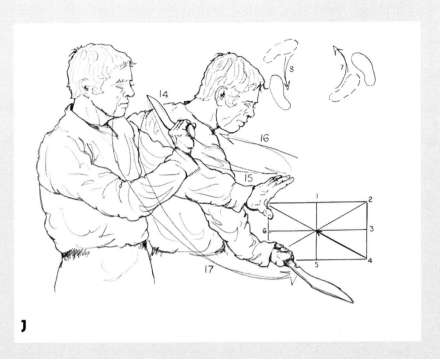

J

K

More on Dealing with the Steel

Action 5: Move the kukri back into an edge-up, point-left position; then slip to an edge-up, point-right position as depicted in drawing L. Immediately execute an angle 6 cut up and across the opponent's thigh, as illustrated in drawing M. Note that movement now shifts from the right to the left. Continue the turn while passing the opponent's arm to your right and follow with an angle 7 attack to his midsection as in drawing N.

L

M

N

Action 6: Move the kukri back into an edge-up, point-right position and follow with an angle 8 attack, as depicted in drawing O.

Note: Remember that the motion for this exercise follows a circular pattern that moves around the target—first to the right, then back to the left. Feel free to execute these cuts from a variety of standing and squatting positions.

O

Training Note 12

Aspects of the Short Strike at Close Quarters

As we discussed in Training Note 10, the short strike can be accomplished with one or two hands, depending on how successful the opponent has been in blocking or disrupting the attack. Most people of normal strength usually will require a two-handed power-assisted cut to overcome an opponent's grip. Whether with one or two hands, short strikes are executed with the weapon arm bent and flexed at the elbow. The cutting attack is usually performed by moving from one chamber into another, as depicted in Figure 186. The short strike cuts arc across and around with a rotation of the hips in the direction of the cut. As the cut is completed, a slight compression of the legs provides additional cutting power.

The narrow rectangular cutting diagram illustrated in Figure 187 provides an approximate view of just how narrow this space can be. Remember, this is just a guide for solo work; the actual cuts may be more circular and even change direction, depending on what the opponent may do to disrupt or block the attack. It is a really good idea to practice the short strike cuts on a regular basis, similar to that illustrated in Figures 188 through 195. Let's take a look.

Figure 186

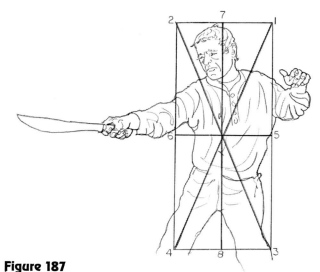

Figure 187

Action 1: Begin by striking down from a high guard into a circular angle 1. As the blade descends, maintain a slight flex as the blade is pulled across the chest into a cross chamber, as shown in Figure 188. This cut normally terminates when the pommel passes over the ribs on the left side of the body. During the course of this cut, the execution of angle footwork left or right can enhance the target opportunity as one moves around the opponent. As the angle 1 cut is completed, the action continues by lifting into a point-up position and back down into an angle 2 circular cut as illustrated in Figure 189. Both the angle 1 and 2 cuts should be performed one after another while maintaining the tight chamber discussed earlier.

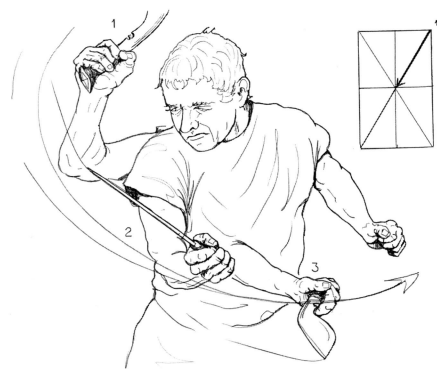

Figure 188

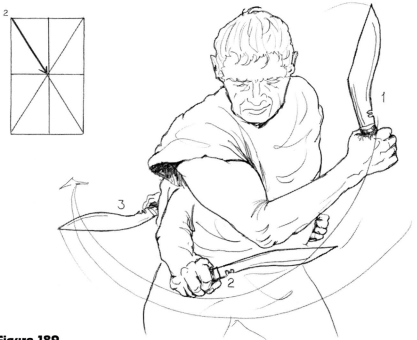

Figure 189

Aspects of the Short Strike at Close Quarters

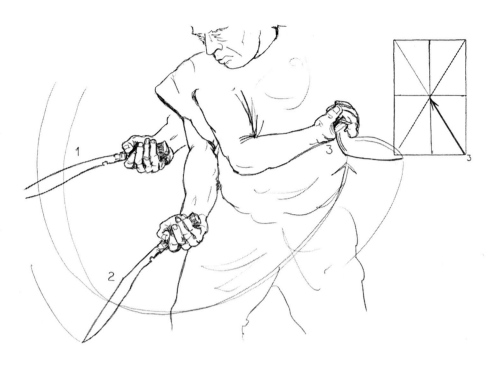

Figure 190

Action 2: As Action 1 is completed, drop the point of the kukri over to the right and down. From this extended position, draw the arm up into a chamber, pulling the blade across the opponent's left thigh in a circular ascending cut into the abdomen, as illustrated in Figure 190. As the angle 3 is completed, pull the blade over toward the left shoulder and into a cross chamber, as illustrated in Figure 191. Pull the blade around and up into the angle 4 ascending circular cut. The angle 3 and 4 cuts should be performed one after another while maintaining the tight chamber discussed earlier.

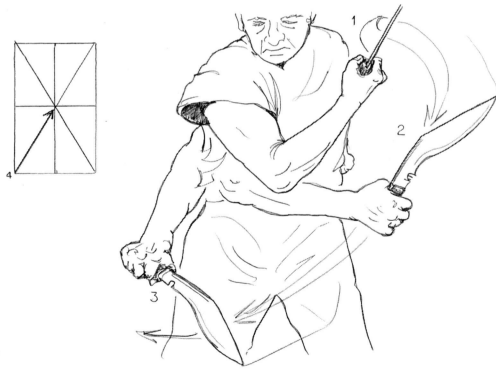

Figure 191

Action 3: On completion of Action 2, drop the kukri point over to the right into a horizontal position and immediately drive the edge to the left into an angle 5 horizontal short strike cut across the opponent's abdomen, as illustrated in Figure 192. When the angle 5 is complete, flip the blade to the left and pull it violently over to the right through an angle 6 horizontal cut, as illustrated in Figure 193.

Figure 192

Figure 193

Aspects of the Short Strike at Close Quarters

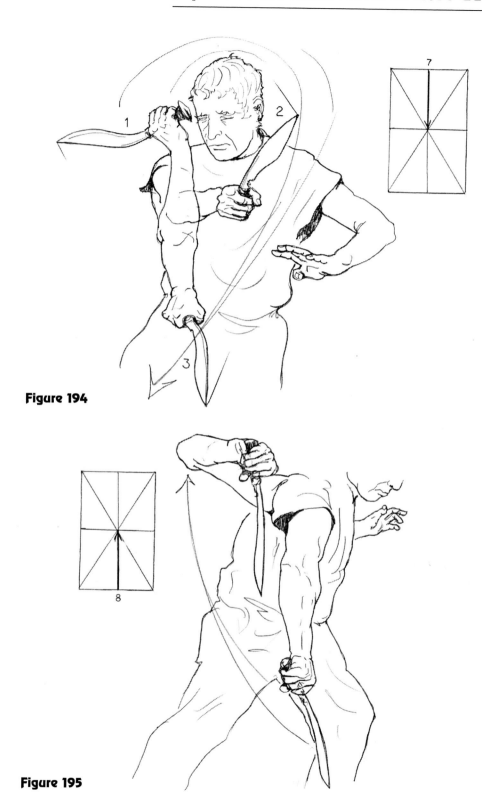

Figure 194

Figure 195

Action 4: As Action 3 is complete, flip the kukri to the left rear and into an edge-up position. Immediately deliver an overhand vertical descending chop to the opponent's head, as illustrated in Figure 194. Retract the kukri and swing it back over to the left rear, arcing into the opponent's groin area. On impact, immediately execute a draw cut up through the opponent's groin and abdomen as shown in Figure 195. These cuts should be performed one after another while maintaining the tight chamber as discussed earlier.

Note: It is recommended that you repeat this cutting pattern a minimum of 10 to 15 times each training period as part of the regular regimen along with the long strike cuts. Remember that each of the actions should be executed in a continuous rhythm, with focus on each cut flowing smoothly into the other. This is just a base exercise—feel free to modify and add additional movement as you see fit. After a sufficient number of solo sets, move on to the heavy or silhouette bag and execute each of the actions at full speed. After this, move on to the pell and run the pattern with live steel.

Using the Two-Handed Block or Closed Triangle as a Two-Handed Punch

As we saw earlier, the shape of the kukri blade lends itself to effective two-handed blocks, levers, and cuts, particularly when the spine is resting against the forearm as illustrated in the drawing at the top of drawing A. It is also effective when used as a two-handed punch during closure with an opponent. This technique is used as part of a leaping action, where the triangle is driven forcefully out and extended into a variety of high and middle-line target areas. The various impact zones of the two-handed punch are depicted in the drawing at the top of drawing A. These start at the pommel, run through the closed fist, and terminate on the recurve. These punches usually are disruptive techniques and are immediately followed by a lever, pommel strike, or cut.

In silat, this type of punch can be enhanced by rotating the weapon hand around to the left, as illustrated at the bottom of drawing A. This approach is called a corkscrew punch (some kung fu systems refer to it as the double punch). When executing these punches, one usually deals with the steel by sidestepping or angling left or right prior to launching. To familiarize ourselves with this, let's use a silhouette bag and training knife.

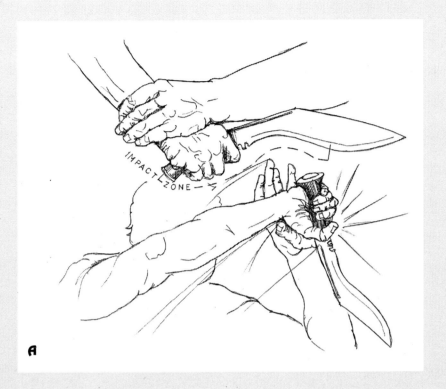

A

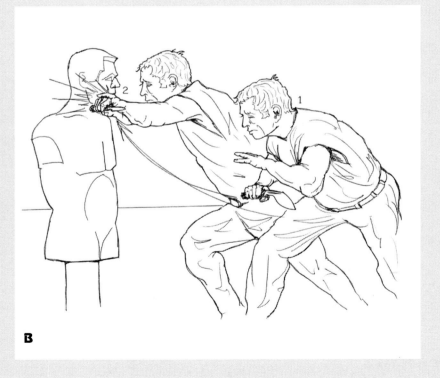

B

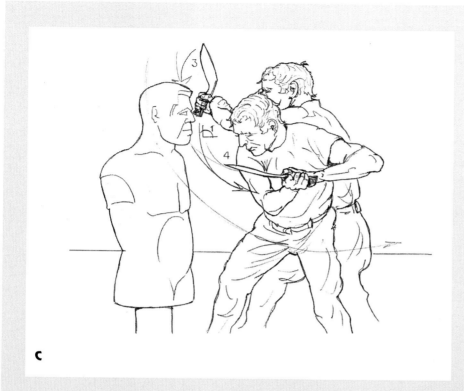

C

D

Action 1: Begin in a low crouch, with the strong-side leg forward. You should be just out of striking range. Visualize your opponent executing a straight thrust to your mid-section, which you counter by sidestepping to your left and launching a two-handed punch into the opponent's throat, as illustrated in drawing B. To enhance this action, consider moving into attack position on the jog. This will give more power and distance to your attack.

Action 2: On impact, lift the kukri point up and to your right and immediately execute a two-handed, power-assisted cut across the opponent's throat, as illustrated in drawing C.

Note: The drawings depicting this action show a bit more separation than should actually be. This is done for clarity so you can see the action. In reality, the actions are much closer!

Action 3: On completion of Action 2, move the kukri up and around and down into a two-handed, power-assisted angle 2 cut, shown in drawing D.

The Fighting Kukri

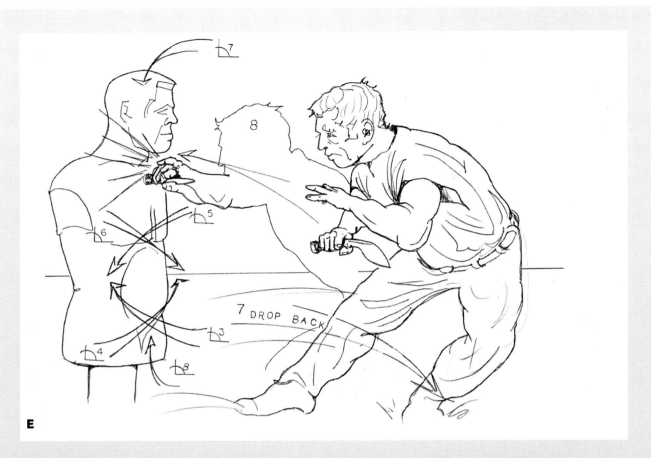

E

Action 4: As the angle 2 is completed, bound backward out of distance and then repeat the closure leap of Action 1, followed by angle 3 and 4 short strike cuts as illustrated in drawing E.

Action 5: Repeat Action 4, only this time follow with angle 5 and 6 short strike cuts.

Action 6: Repeat Action 4, only this time follow with angle 7 and 8 short strike cuts.

Note: Keep in mind as you practice these closure actions that this is not just a "mad rush" into your opponent. You must deal with the steel by avoiding or pinning his weapon. It is also a good idea to practice this on the swinging bag, as we addressed earlier.

Training Note 13 Aspects of Hand-on-Hand

In Training Note 12, we placed a lot of focus on rapid closure to deal with the steel. Now let's move to the next logical event, where the two-hand punch is checked and you and your opponent have come to grips. Basically, he has hold of your weapon arm at the wrist and you have his, as illustrated in the bottom drawing of Figure 196. This position was likely a more common eventuality in fights of the eighteenth and nineteenth centuries than the dueling scenario of movies and stage combat.

In these clinches, both fighters attempt to control the weapon arm. It may be necessary to slide the hand forward onto the opponent's hand at positions A, B, and C illustrated in the top drawing of Figure 196. This is a force-on-force struggle, where the arms may move back and forth or up and down, as conceptualized in Figure 197. This creates a situation that I've come to call "the moment in time." Here we anticipate the opponent's move by *feeling* the pressure he exerts against any action you take to escape his grip.

Let's look at the example depicted in Figure 198. In step 1, you push against the opponent's grip with your weapon arm. When this occurs, most opponents

Figure 196

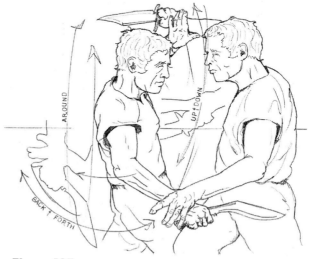

Figure 197

will instinctively begin pushing back or forcefully resisting the push, as seen in step 2. When you feel this pressure, drop your blade point to an edge-up position and begin an angle left step while ripping the kukri free and into an immediate cut to the opponent's wrist, as shown in steps 3 and 4. Simultaneously pull the opponent's weapon arm down with a twist to the wrist. The opponent should tilt to his left to maintain balance; when he does, execute an angle 8 cut to the groin.

This "moment in time" occurs when you first feel the opponent's pressure and should be executed as rapidly as possible, not allowing him time to react. Now let's look at some common techniques that can be used to achieve this.

Figure 198

THE CIRCULAR RELEASE

One of the techniques that stuck with me over the years, from W. Hoch Hochheim's Expert Knife Program, is what some call the circular release. This aspect begins when opponents lock up in a hand-on-hand situation as addressed in the scenario above. As soon as this occurs, the goal is to get your weapon free and into action with one of the short strike cuts or thrusts

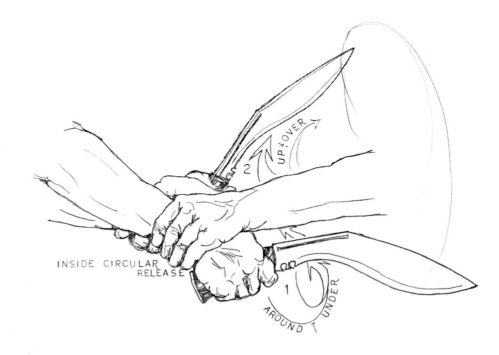

Figure 199

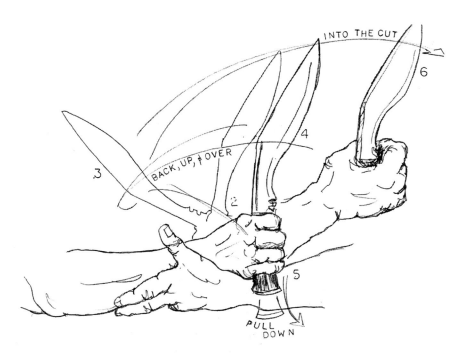

Figure 200

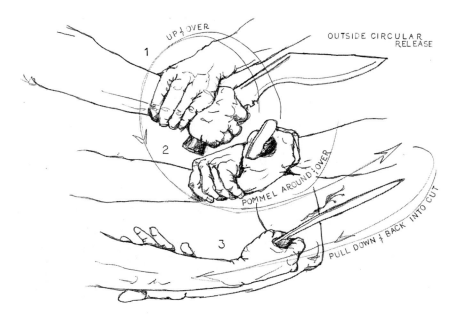

Figure 201

described earlier. The inside and outside circular releases are two common ways to achieve this, often in combination with kicks, stomps, and knee strikes.

Inside Circular Release

To execute this technique, assume the opponent has gripped your wrist in a palms-down overhand grip, as illustrated in Figure 199. As soon as you are grabbed, execute a slight pull to your rear. When you feel the opponent pull back or push forward, drop the point of the kukri around and under his forearm, as shown in step 1 of Figure 199. As soon as your point rises on the other side of his forearm, rotate your wrist around to the left, then up and over as illustrated in step 2. As illustrated in steps 3 and 4 of Figure 200, begin to rotate the wrist to your right until the pommel drops over the opponent's forearm. Immediately pull down and then push out into a cut, as shown in steps 5 and 6.

Outside Circular Release

This technique rotates the spine of the kukri back up and over, as illustrated in step 1 of Figure 201. Rotate the pommel around and over the top of the opponent's wrist. Then pull back immediately, effecting a cut on the opponent's arm or rib cage as depicted in steps 2 and 3 of the figure.

Counter to the Inside and Outside Circular Release

The counter to this technique is basically the same for both releases. It involves dropping and rotating the hand down and around the opponent's weapon wrist and into a palm-up grip. This is a quick, snap-like action that is executed as soon as you feel the opponent's wrist begin to rotate, as illustrated in Figure 202.

CLOSING AND WORKING THE CIRCULAR RELEASE

Now let's do some work escaping from the hand-on-hand situation. We'll work with a training partner, starting slow and progressing to medium and full speed as proficiency increases. The emphasis here will be on intercepting and grabbing the opponent's weapon hand and then executing one of the circular releases to get your weapon into action. For this exercise, we will use protective eyewear, groin protection, and wrist and elbow pads. As before, for the purpose of clarity these will not be shown in the illustrations. Begin by facing your partner at a distance of about 10 feet in a middle or high guard position.

Action 1: The trainees

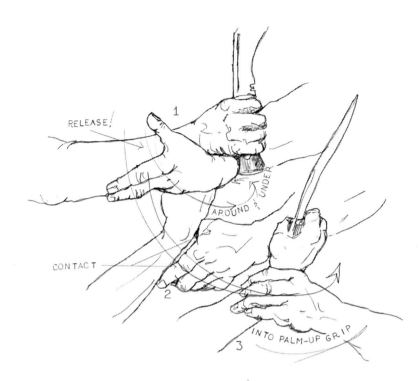

Figure 202

Figure 203

rapidly close the distance, as shown in Figure 203. As they close, partner 1 grabs partner 2's weapon arm, as depicted in Figure 204.

Action 2: Partner 2 grabs and secures partner 1's wrist, as seen in Figure 205, and both exercise in a "moment in time" positioning.

Action 3: Partner 1 executes an outside circular release, as depicted in Figure 206. Immediately, partner 2 executes his outside circular release. Both partners disengage and move back out of the close-quarter range.

Action 4: Both partners close the distance again, repeating the same steps as in Actions 1 and 2.

Action 5: Both partners take turns executing outside and inside circular releases as in Action 3.

Action 6: Repeat Actions 1 through 5, only this time each partner executes the counters to the circular release.

Figure 204

Figure 205

WORKING THE TWO-HANDED BLOCK IN CLOSE

Picking up again with the two-handed block, here is a partner exercise that can be worked at close range. Begin by facing your training partner at medium range. Extend your left arm and walk forward until you can place your hand on his shoulder, as illustrated in Figure 207. This is the close-quarter range that will be used until you become familiar with the technique. Later, when you are comfortable with the technique, the actual distance illustrated in Figure 208 can be used.

The focus of this exercise is simply to execute the two-handed block and then close either inside or outside to effect a two-handed cut. Initially, your partner will deliver short strike cuts with a single hand. As proficiency improves, he should switch to the two-handed cut. Both partners should use wooden or carbon fiber training weapons and wear hand, forearm, elbow, and eye protection. Because close-quarter techniques with limited space are difficult to illustrate, the drawings depict much more distance than would actually be the case. As with the other exercises, begin slowly and gradually increase speed

Figure 206

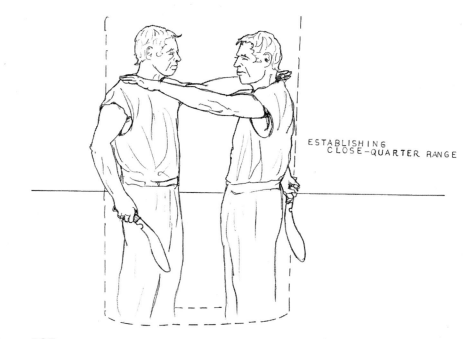

Figure 207

166

Aspects of Hand-on-Hand

Figure 208

until you are comfortable at faster engagements. Remember that your partner is serving as a training aid—this is not a competition.

Action 1: Partner 1 begins the exercise by executing an angle 1 short strike to the left side of partner 2's neck. Beginning in a middle guard, partner 2 executes a two-handed block and angle right footwork, as illustrated in Figure 209.

Figure 209

Action 2: Partner 1 pulls back and immediately executes an angle 2 cut to the right side of partner 2's neck, who immediately executes a two-handed block to the right as shown in Figure 210.

Action 3: Partner 1 pivots to the left and pulls his weapon back and around into an angle 3 cut to the legs of partner 2, as shown in Figure 211. Partner 2 counters with a low line, two-handed block while executing angle right footwork.

Figure 210

Figure 211

Action 4: Partner 1 rolls his kukri to the left across his chest and into an immediate angle 4 short strike cut to partner 2's right leg. Partner 2 follows with a two-handed block to his right, as shown in Figure 212.

Action 5: Partner 1 pivots to his right while pulling the kukri across his chest to the right into an immediate angle 5 chop to the midsection of Partner 2. Partner 2 counters with a two-handed block to his left, as illustrated in Figure 213.

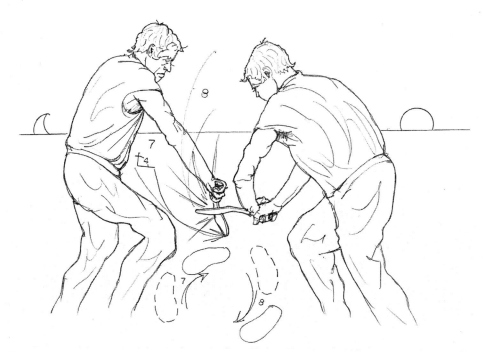

Figure 212

Figure 213

Action 6: Partner 1 flips his kukri point to the left and executes an angle 6 short strike cut to the right side of partner 2. Partner 2 counters with a two-handed block to his right, as depicted in Figure 214.

Note: This is a simple base exercise whose structure can be enhanced with additional techniques for the elbow and hand, as well as with an assortment of pinning, passing, pulling, and pushing moves. Try to execute this exercise in one continuous flow, with one action transitioning smoothly into the other. Throughout the exercise, look and feel for additional openings.

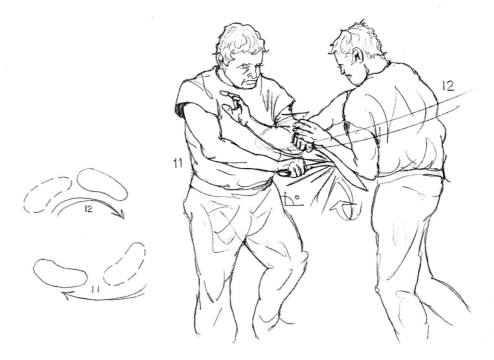

Figure 214

Training Note 14 Aspects of the Jurus

Back in the late 1990s, I devoted considerable time to composing a bowie and big knife curriculum for my School of Two Swords. The techniques were nothing remarkable in that I borrowed heavily from a variety of sources, both past and present, historic and modern. You will find these addressed in my text *Advanced Bowie Techniques*. Because most of the curriculum was focused on medium range, some people considered it to be "dueling."

After a period of time, I began to search for a martial system that would address the close-quarter fight and be conceptual enough for easy adaptability to big knives. I was first exposed to silat by Guru Brandt Smith of the Boxing Brotherhood at a seminar at my home on the use of the Indonesian tribal blade called the *kujang*. The five jurus associated with that weapon stuck in my mind for their simplicity and applicability to both medium and close range using both saber and reverse grip. Some of these you will recognize in my two bowie books.

Around the same time, I ran across a remarkable training support package put out by Joseph Simonet. The package consisted of two videos and a book titled *Silat Concepts, Form and Function*. Due to the diversity of my interests and the demands of careers in the military and civil service, I never had the opportunity to receive any long-term training in silat. Simonet's book and videos helped me fill the gaps, giving me a conceptual base to enhance both my personal training and curriculum in silat, while opening the door to my understanding the close-quarter fight.

Simonet's work focuses on the first six jurus of the pentjak silat serak system and presents his take on the conceptual application of this secretive martial system. Jurus are not unlike kata or forms—they provide the structural movements associated with the combative techniques. You might say that it is a method of organizing the material for the mind. Simonet's analogy of the juru being the penmanship for learning the silat system caught my attention, and it was not long before I was seeing the applications to a variety of weapons.

When I began to train with the kukri, I quickly realized that these six simple jurus just might be the key or base from which to teach its applications. What you are going to see in this training note is *my take* on the application of the jurus in Simonet's book to the kukri. It is a conceptual approach and is only one of the many possibilities that can be gleaned from studying the jurus with a kukri in your hand. I want to sincerely thank Joseph Simonet and his partner Addy Hernandez for the clarity of their instruction and for making this training support package available.

THE TRACE OF THE JURU

Jurus, like kata or forms, are an ancient martial art training technique that arose during a time when a large percentage of the world's population could not read or write. It was also a period before the widespread availability of printed material, when knowledge was captured for a select few on handwritten manuscripts. A juru is nothing more than a "word of mouth" method of passing on training objectives and techniques to the student of a specific martial system.

Today, this approach to training has critics in the self-defense community, primarily because it has evolved into a competitive sport that is characterized by expansive dance and gymnastic elements. Kata has morphed more into a literal "martial art" than a combative system. This is not the case with the juru, which remains the first step in learning the practical application of the techniques of silat. The juru is the structure that stimulates the memory of the flow of the technique. It is the essence of solo training and allows one to actively visualize the actions of an opponent. For me, this far outweighs any negative aspects. It is just part of the cycle of combat training that allows one to train without a partner or instructor. Most important, it allows you to experience how the geometry of movement—such as the circles, angles, and lines—all flow in and out of our reactions to the cues our opponent sends us.

USING THE JURU IN THIS TEXT

To adapt the kukri to the juru, I have selected three of the original six that were included in Joseph Simonet's *Silat Concepts, Form and Function*. I have illustrated these in two sets of drawings: one depicting the *flow* of the juru and a second showing the *application* with a training partner. Begin by first learning the flow as a solo set, to be practiced in front of a wall chart, mirror, or just alone in the open air. As you go through the various actions, attempt to visualize an actual opponent attacking you with a variety of cuts, thrusts, and short strikes

inside that close-quarter circle we addressed in chapter 5. Once you have committed the juru to memory, practice it on a heavy bag, where you can experience applying the juru while moving inside and outside the box against an opponent. Don't forget to change the elevation by moving from high to low-line target areas in a continuous flowing attack. Work the juru outside on a variety of terrain and under all sorts of weather conditions while experimenting with adjusting the footwork patterns to accommodate traction on different slopes and surfaces. Finally, begin partner training with the juru, using both a cooperative and resisting opponent.

The Flow for Juru 1

Action 1: Begin in a middle guard position as shown in the drawing on the right of Figure 215. Visualize an opponent making a mad rush forward to pin your weapon arm. At this cue, slide back and execute an angle right step to take your body out of the line of attack. As you move, rotate the weapon arm up and around to your right and into position for an angle 5 cut.

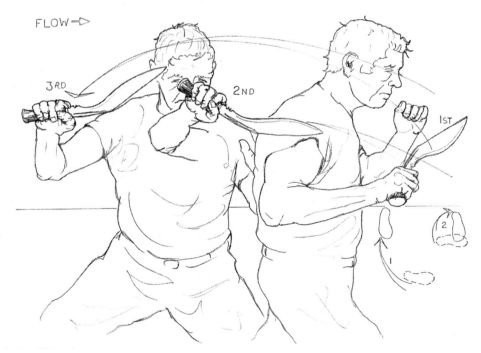

Figure 215

Figure 216

Action 2: As you visualize the opponent rushing by, slide forward and deliver an angle 5 cut to his midsection, illustrated in Figure 216.

Action 3: Immediately following the cut, raise the arms and hands into a two-handed grip and deliver a high-line elbow strike with the left arm as illustrated in Figure 217. Follow immediately with an elbow or pommel strike with the right arm.

Figure 217

Action 4: As the elbow strike is completed, immediately disengage the weapon hand and move it up and into a two-handed angle 7 cut. As the cut is delivered, drop down on one knee while continuing to cut into the abdomen through the groin, shown in Figure 218. As the angle 7 cut is completed, flip the blade to an edge-up position and execute an angle 8 cut through the opponent's inside thigh while moving back to a standing position.

Figures 219 through 223 illustrate the application of juru 1 with a training partner. Remember, these drawings are somewhat conceptual and do not depict the proper safety equipment for the head, hand, wrist, elbow, arm, groin, and eyes that must me worn.

Figure 218

Figure 219

Aspects of the Jurus

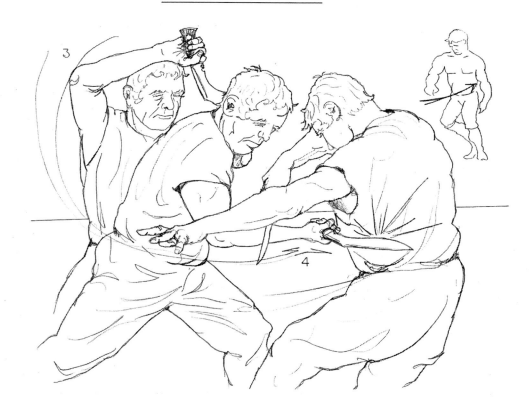

Figure 220

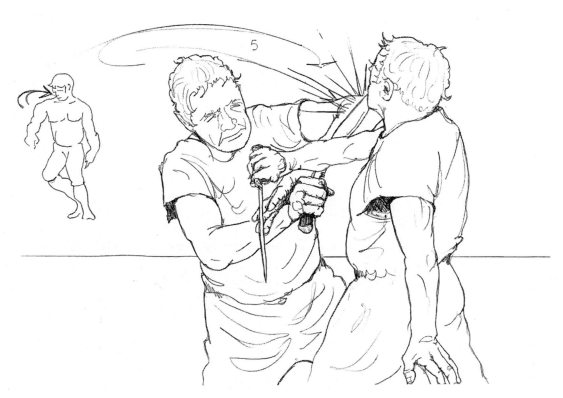

Figure 221

The Fighting Kukri

Figure 222

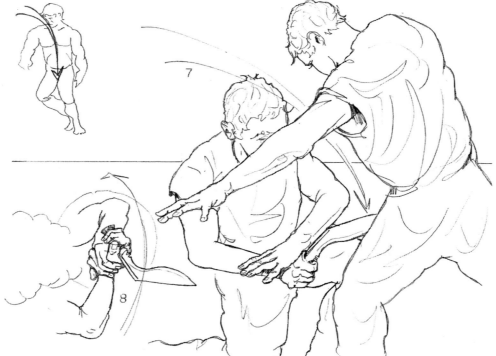

Figure 223

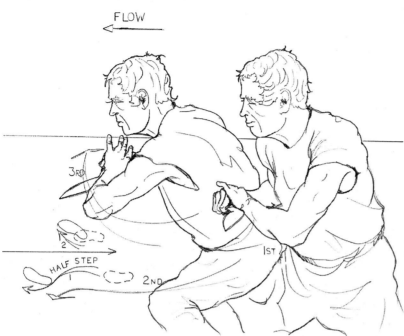

Figure 224

The Flow for Juru 2

Action 1: Begin with a middle guard and two-handed grip as shown in Figure 224. Visualize an opponent rapidly closing and delivering a straight thrust to your midsection. As the thrust comes in, half step outside to the left to avoid the attack.

Action 2: Before the opponent can retract his weapon arm, drive forward with a two-handed punch/block into his throat or chin, as illustrated in Figure 225. Depending on the location of the opponent's weapon arm, drop the kukri point down or up to hook the arm with the pommel, as shown on the left of Figure 225 and completed in Figure 226 with a pass of the opponent's arm.

Figure 225

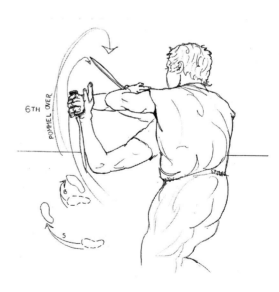

Figure 226

Action 3: Visualize having to repeat the process in Action 2, except that you hook and pass the opponent's arm to the left as shown in Figure 227. On completion, execute an angle 2 cut to the opponent's neck.

Action 4: Visualize the opponent checking your angle 2 cut with his empty hand. On contact, flip the blade to your right around the blocking hand and step away to the left, executing an angle 1 cut to either the hand or neck as visualized in Figure 228.

Figures 229 through 232 illustrate the application of juru 2 with a training partner. In this case, the opponent's arm is only passed once before detecting the opening and delivering a cut.

Figure 227

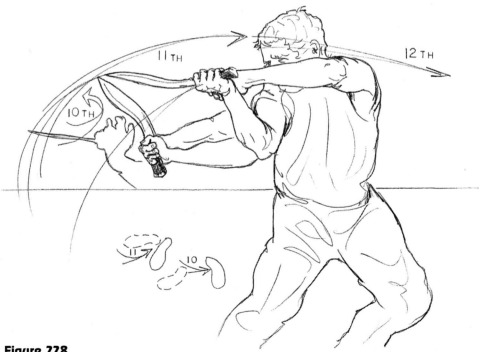

Figure 228

Aspects of the Jurus

APPLICATION

THRUST

SIDE STEP

Figure 229

TWO-HAND PUNCH 2

Figure 230

179

The Fighting Kukri

Figure 231

Figure 232

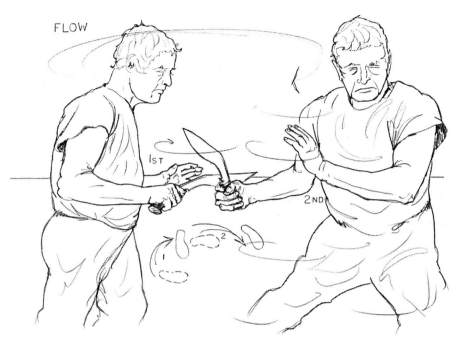

Figure 233

The Flow for Juru 3

Action 1: Beginning in a middle guard position, visualize an opponent rushing in and attempting to trap your weapon arm. As the opponent nears, sidestep to your left as illustrated in Figure 233.

Action 2: As the opponent closes, drop to one knee and execute an angle 6 chop to his knee. On contact, rotate the blade to the left and execute a power-assisted angle 4 cut up through the abdomen and ribs, as drawn in Figure 234.

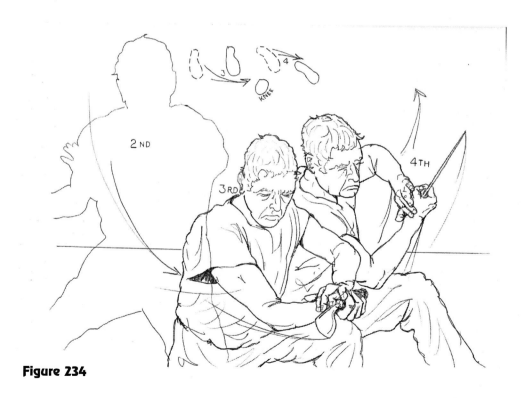

Figure 234

The Fighting Kukri

Action 3: On completion of Action 2, flip the blade over and execute an angle 1 cut back through the opponent's arms or midsection. As the cut is completed, move up to a standing position while stepping around to the opponent's rear, as depicted in Figure 235.

Action 4: As you step around to the opponent's back, flip the kukri to an edge-down position and execute an angle 7 cut down the length of his spine, as shown in Figure 236.

Figures 237 through 240 illustrate the application of juru 3 with a training partner.

Note: The goal when working the juru as a solo set is to execute each technique in one continuous flow.

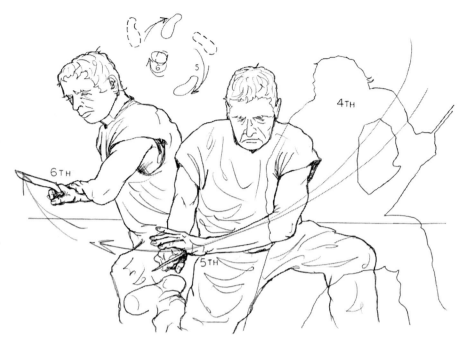

Figure 235

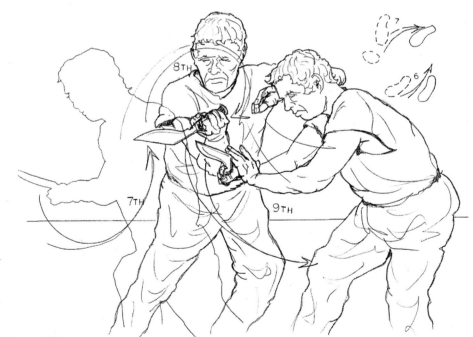

Figure 236

Aspects of the Jurus

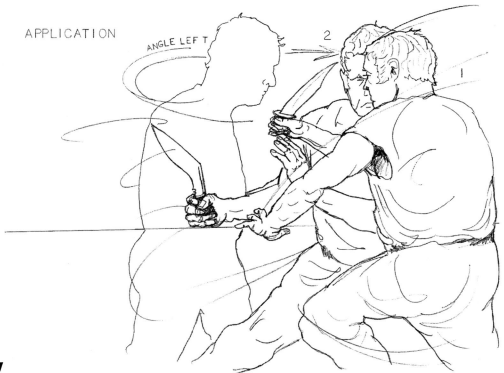

Figure 237

Figure 238

The Fighting Kukri

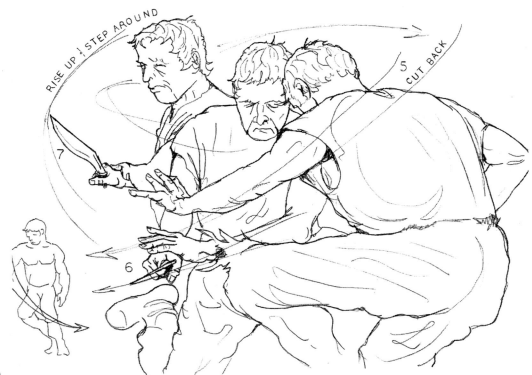

Figure 239

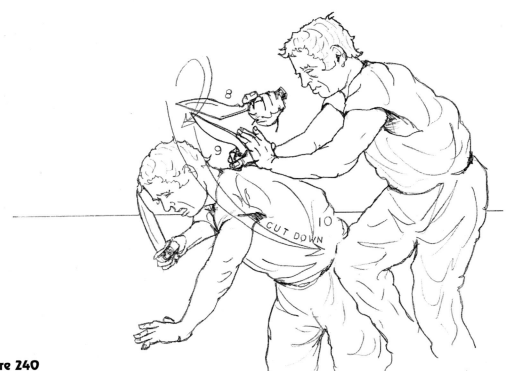

Figure 240

184

Aspects of the Jurus

ASPECTS OF THE KUJANG JURUS

As memory serves, it was the summer of 2002 when Guru Brandt Smith agreed to swap instruction at a seminar at my home. Part of the deal was that I would show him my bowie knife material and he

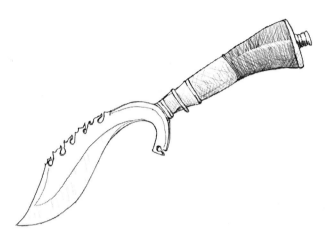

Figure 241

Figure 242

would teach a block of instruction on a unique weapon that originated in the Pasundan (Sundanese) region of Western Java. This weapon was called the *kujang* (illustrated in Figure 241). Like the bowie and kukri, the kujang had humble origins as a working tool that over time evolved into a weapon of myth and mystery. Although the kujang originates from the Hindu culture, it eventually fell under the influence of Islamic religious traditions.

It is said that the kujang was consecrated with magical powers whose blade design symbolically represented the shape of the island of Java. Early designs had three holes along the spine, which represented the three aspects of the Hindu religion. Later designs developed under Muslim influence acquired five holes to represent the five pillars of Islam. I am not going to go any further into the history, origin, and techniques of the unique kujang other than to say that it is for another writing at another time in the dim future.

I am afraid that Brandt got the short end of the stick in terms of information exchange at our seminar. I was so enamored with the six jurus he had adapted to the kujang that I did more learning than teaching. As a continuation of our close-quarter work in this book, I've included two of those six jurus we learned that remarkable day. They are just as applicable to the kukri as they are to the kujang. Along with the jurus I discussed earlier, this will give the reader five total jurus for exploring the conceptual aspect with the kukri.

Aspects of Kujang Juru 1
Action 1: Beginning in a middle guard, visualize an opponent executing a straight thrust to your midsection. While moving with an angle right step, execute a point-down parry as illustrated in Figure 242. Immediately follow by

185

reaching under and grabbing the opponent's wrist, as illustrated in Figure 243. Twist the wrist to your left as you slide forward and deliver an angle 6 horizontal cut to the neck.

Action 2: Visualize the opponent blocking your cut with his left hand. Immediately, release his wrist and wrap your arm around and over into a snaking lock that puts pressure on the elbow. Pull the opponent into your left side while flipping the kukri over into a fingers-up position as illustrated in Figure 244.

Figure 243

Figure 244

Aspects of the Jurus

Figure 245

Action 3: While still securing the opponent's weapon arm, reach over and grab your right wrist and execute a power-assisted angle 7 cut down through the opponent's face, neck, and groin, as illustrated in Figure 245. During this action, drive your hips down into a squat or kneeling position to add force to the cut.

Action 4: From the squat, flip the kukri to a pommel-up position, as illustrated in Figure 246; then immediately execute a power-assisted angle 8 cut back along the same line as Action 3.

Figure 246

Aspects of Kujang Juru 2

Action 1: Beginning in a low guard position, visualize your opponent executing an angle 6 cut to your right side. Using the footwork pattern at the upper left of Figure 247, slide to your right and execute an edge-down block on the incoming blade. Follow with a forearm strike to the opponent's arm.

Action 2: From a position outside the box, execute a fingers-down thrust to the opponent's neck, as shown in Figure 248. Immediately roll the kukri edge to the left while reaching up into a two-handed grip, as depicted in Figure 249. Slide forward

Figure 247

Figure 248

Figure 249

to the left and execute a power-assisted angle 1 cut across the opponent's throat and chest.

Action 3: On completion of action 2, immediately drive the kukri back up with a two-handed, power-assisted thrust into the opponent's neck, as seen in Figure 250. Immediately step to your right and execute a second two-handed angle 1 cut down across the arm and hip, as illustrated in Figure 251. Immediately raise back to a standing position while executing an edge-up, power-assisted cut as shown in Figure 252.

Figure 250

Figure 251

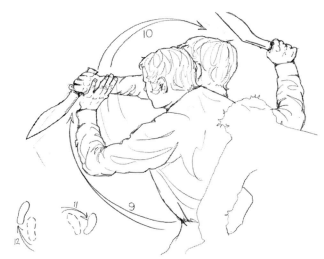

Figure 252

The Fighting Kukri

Since most of the practical applications are similar to the other jurus, I have not included drawings of actions with a training partner.

Any of the jurus can be linked together to form a longer, more dynamic solo set that exercises both footwork and the cardio aspect of your training. This is especially true for the kujang juru. I suggest you experiment with these to develop your own unique kukri sets.

Training Note 15 Adding the Kicks

There are vast numbers of books, videos, and websites that can teach the fundamentals of kicking much better than I can. Because of my physical limitations and old injuries, I tend to keep kicks below the belt line of the opponent, leaving those graceful high-line kicks to those whose core martial art places focus in that approach. I will use the term "kicks" to apply generically to a variety of leg and foot techniques that complement any of the engagement sets shown in this text. These are used to attack the lower limbs when the opponent's focus is occupied on the high line. In this low-line area, kicks are traditionally delivered with the ball or heel of the foot, while leg sweeps use the top of the foot or heel, as illustrated in Figure 253. The toe kick is usually not delivered without wearing footwear that has a rigid sole and top, such as boots or sturdy shoes.

For our purposes, we will address three kicking techniques for medium range and three for the hand-on-hand, close-quarter engagement. For medium range, we will discuss the "through-the-heart" kick, the toe kick, and the side kick. At close quarters, although not specifically kicks, the leg sweep, the stomp, and knee strikes will be addressed. The targets for the kicking methods are illustrated in Figure 254. We will refer back to these periodically throughout our discussion.

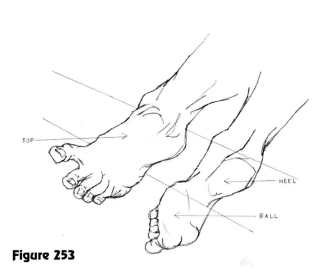

Figure 253

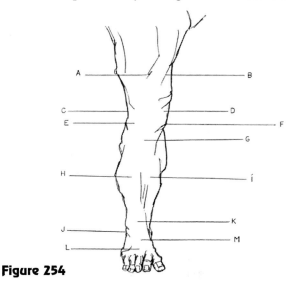

Figure 254

BALANCE AND THE CENTER OF GRAVITY

In some martial systems, there is a tendency to think of the kick as the primary attack mode for working both inside and outside the box. The focus is usually on targeting and looking for those openings similar to what we have addressed in the earlier training notes. While this is a valid approach, the aspects of *balance* and the opponent's *center of gravity* must also be considered to produce an efficient kick that will stop incoming movement and eventually lead to toppling an attacker to the ground. For me, I do not see the kick as being an end within itself but rather a complement to the weapon techniques. By its disruptive nature, a kick can create openings and distract the opponent. That said, let's look at a method for adding balance and the center of gravity to our training methods.

One cannot talk about a center of gravity without addressing balance between opposing and counteracting forces. The center of gravity does not change without the balance changing. This is why we as bipeds are able to walk, run, and jump without falling down. Basically, the feet, legs, and arms assist in providing balance no matter where the head and torso are. Whether one is leaning forward or back, left or right, on one foot or two, the balance in relation to the center of gravity is working against a variety of gravity-applied angular forces to keep us upright. Any student of judo, wrestling, and push hands deals with these elements on a regular basis during training.

I first became aware of this aspect after spending a lot of hours in anatomical drawing classes. Here,

illustrating the point of balance and the appropriate center of gravity was used as a means of imparting motion and action when illustrating the human body. The same is true for the martial arts, where they take on the form of a cue for destabilizing an opponent. The internationally known artist and instructor George Bridgman described the center of gravity as an imaginary line that begins at the neck and runs through the leg that supports the weight. Drawing A of Figure 255 illustrates the center of gravity with the weight placed on the leading leg and the balance maintained on the ball of the foot. To unbalance an opponent, there is a rule of thumb that says to kick the leg bearing the weight and sweep the one that is not. This is not an absolute but rather rests with the power one is able to generate with one's legs.

Another aspect of the center of gravity is that it shifts to the center when the weight is equally distributed on both feet, as shown by the dashed line in Figure 255, drawing A. These cues are acquired

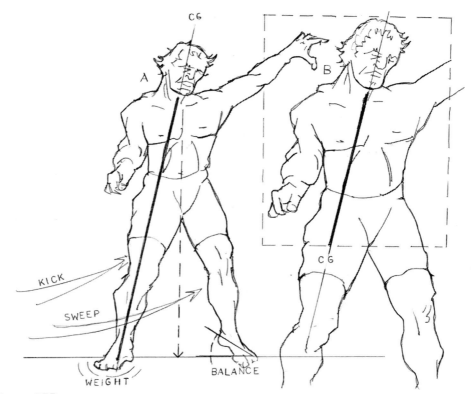

Figure 255

Adding the Kicks

Figure 256

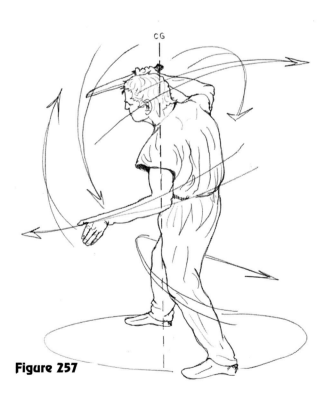

Figure 257

visually at medium range; however at close-quarter range, it becomes a matter of *feeling* the opponent's balance, with the visual cues limited to the area illustrated by the dashed box in drawing B.

Figure 256 illustrates another example of how center of gravity and balance work together. Here, prior to delivering a cut, an opponent delivers a side kick typically seen in Thai boxing. Note how the center of gravity shifts off to angle X1, with the weight bearing on the right leg to maintain balance. If you were to shift to his left and kick his right leg supporting the weight, it would disrupt his cut and possibly open his guard for an immediate counterattack with your kukri. This is a classic example of how a counter kick can disrupt the opponent's attack without actually waiting for his weapon to come in. Another method is to create an opening, launch a high-line attack, then follow with a kick to the low-line area. You might say this is the *rhythm* of when one should kick/sweep at medium range.

Remember I said that at close-quarter, hand-on-hand distance, the center of gravity and balance of an opponent must be *felt* rather than seen? At this distance you really can't see the opponent's feet and upper leg movements. In Figure 257 I have attempted to illustrate the forces of balance that can be applied within this world of close quarters. I was first exposed to this by a Chinese push-hand instructor who said that the focus was on manipulating these forces back and forth and side to side within the close-quarter circle. It is probably best to explain this with an example.

193

Let's assume that our opponent will give cues to his intent, similar to what's shown in Figure 258. In the drawing on the left, he shifts his center of gravity to his right and pushes his hand forward to an 11 o'clock position. You will feel that right leg move toward you and, when accompanied by a push, you can bet his left rear leg is not carrying the weight. In this situation, you can stomp his foot or pull him forward in the direction of his force and execute a rear sweep to his right leg. If he moves back to the center, as in the middle drawing, both arms may push forward or pull you back while his torso becomes centered. In this case, where his base is solid, it might be best to deliver a knee to the groin to unbalance or force him to move. The drawing on the right shows the center of gravity moving to the 1 o'clock position. This is handled similar to the cue for the 11th o'clock drawing.

Figure 258

WORKING WITH BALANCE AND CENTER OF GRAVITY IN A HAND-ON-HAND MODE

You may want to practice this exercise on a really good wrestling or gym mat that will cushion any possi-

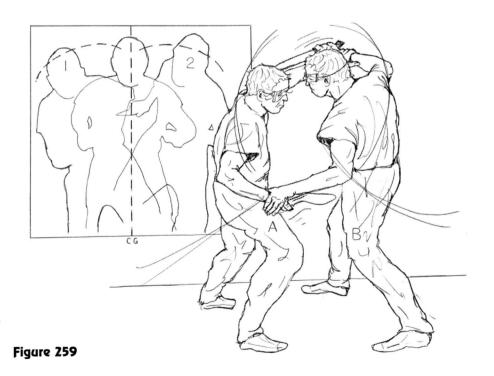

Figure 259

ble falls. I've seen this done really well in a sand or saw dust pit, too. As always, it is a good idea to use eye and groin protection and training weapons.

Designate which partner will be the opponent giving the cues shown in Figure 258. Begin by assuming the hand-on-hand position shown in Figure 259. The first objective is to experience feeling the opponent's balance and knowing when to disrupt it based on the cues he gives. Start off at slow speed and eventually progress to quicker work.

Here is an example of how this should work. Begin with partner A executing cue 1 and leaning in while pushing your hand to the rear. (Again, use moderate resistance till you both get the concept.) Partner B resists the tendency to push back and goes with the opponent's force by pulling back with his left hand and pushing out with his weapon arm. Simultaneously, he twists the opponent's weapon arm, toppling him to his left. Experiment with this at both high and middle-line levels, moving back and forth between the two cues. After both partners have mas-

tered this, begin by inserting low-force kicks and sweeps to assist in the toppling action.

REVIEWING THE KICKING TECHNIQUES

Here is a quick run-through of the kicking techniques, along with some applications used in conjunction with the kukri. First we will present the medium-range applications and follow with the close-quarter aspects.

Through-the-Heart Kick

This kick is executed by first raising the knee, then forcefully driving the heel into the opponent's legs or midsection, as illustrated in Figure 260. This powerful technique is frequently used inside the box and is particularly effective in stopping an opponent's mad rush by driving into his lead knee. The raising action of the knee can also be used to block incoming kicks to the low line. Figures 261 through 264 depict a low-line application of this kick.

Figure 260

Action 1: The opponents close to medium range, as illustrated in Figure 261.

Action 2: Opponent B slides forward and executes a straight thrust to opponent's A midsection. Immediately, opponent A executes an angle right step while parrying the incoming thrust off the centerline, as shown in Figure 262.

Figure 261

Figure 262

Adding the Kicks

Action 3: As B attempts to disengage, opponent A leaps up and to his left, as shown in Figure 263. As he drops down, he drives a through-the-heart kick into the right side of B's leg, as shown in Figure 264. Before B can recover, A delivers a thrust into his back.

Figure 263

Figure 264

The Toe Kick

Figure 265 illustrates the toe kick, which is delivered in a similar manner to the through-the-heart kick. The knee is driven forcefully up and the toe is snapped forward. As mentioned earlier, this technique is best performed with some form of footwear that protects the toes from injury. On impact, it is immediately retracted back to the chambered position rather than to the floor. This kick can be performed with either the forward or rear leg. While not a particularly powerful kick, it can damage the groin or kidney areas. Figures 266 through 269 provide a classic example of the use of the toe kick.

Action 1: Opponent A initiates a straight thrust to opponent B's midsection. B executes an angle left step and drives a point-down parry to deflect the incoming blade, as illustrated in Figure 266.

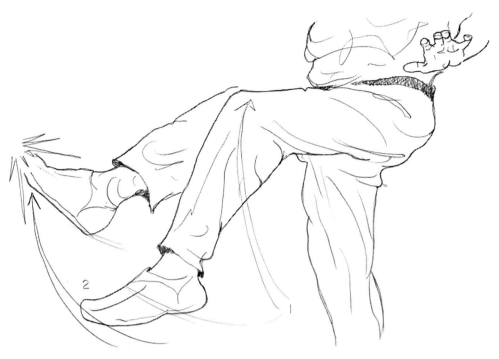

Figure 265

Figure 266

Adding the Kicks

Action 2: As A's blade is pushed off line, B reaches under and grabs his opponent's weapon arm, as shown in Figure 267. After pulling A to his left, B executes a toe kick to the groin, as shown in Figure 268.

Figure 267

Figure 268

The Fighting Kukri

Action 3: Before A can recover, B delivers an angle 2 cut to his throat as shown in Figure 269.

The Side Kick

This kick involves chambering the knee up and the foot to the side. From there it is driven out, impacting on either the ball or the heel. Figure 270 shows this technique. This method works well off a variety of footwork patterns that first begin by moving out of the way of an incoming attack. Figure 271 illustrates this to the low line against an onrushing opponent. Another example is shown in Figures 272 through 273.

Figure 269

Figure 270

Adding the Kicks

Action 1: Opponent A begins by delivering an angle 1 cut while opponent B avoids by executing an angle left step. Immediately, B executes a snap cut to the opponent's incoming hand, as shown in Figure 272.

Figure 271

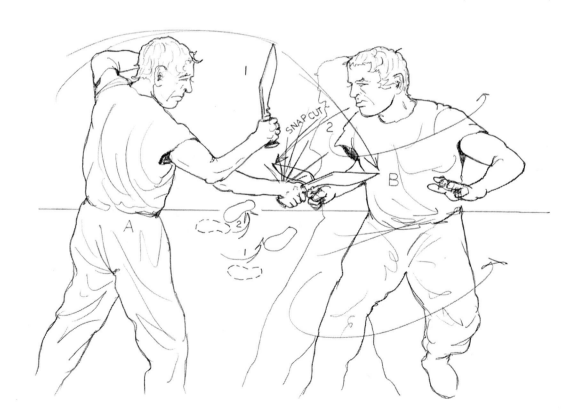

Figure 272

Action 2: Before A can recover, B slides forward and delivers a side kick to the lead knee, as seen in Figure 273.

The Sweep

This technique is usually best executed at close range, when you and your opponent have come to grips and are manipulating each other's center of gravity and balance. It involves hooking the top of the foot or the heel around the opponent's ankle or lower leg, as shown in Figure 274. Other targets for the sweep shown in Figure 254 are at J, K, or M. When the top of the foot is used, it is termed a forward sweep; with the heel, it is a reverse sweep.

Figure 273

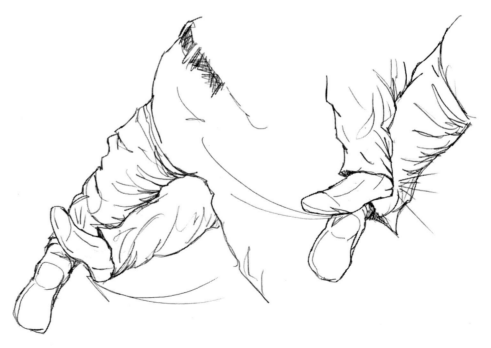

Figure 274

Adding the Kicks

The Stomp

This approach involves driving the heel and arch of the foot down onto targets M, J, K, H, I, G, or E, depending on the angle of attack. The intent with the stomp is to put force against the joints at an angle opposite of the natural bend of the leg. This action usually will force the opponent to move in order to maintain balance. The example in Figures 275 and 276 illustrates a stomp being used in conjunction with a sweep. In most cases, when you step on the top of an opponent's foot, his instinct will be to pull the foot back while shifting his weight to the opposite leg. As soon as this is felt, bring the opposite leg across and deliver a sweep to unbalance the opponent. Another example of the sweep/stomp combination is illustrated in Figures 277 through 278.

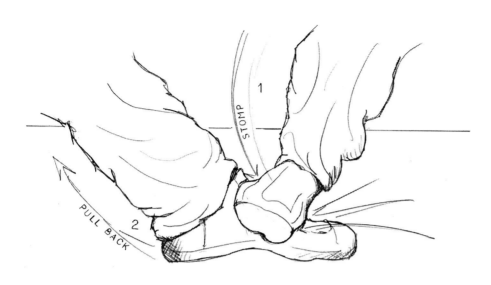

Figure 275

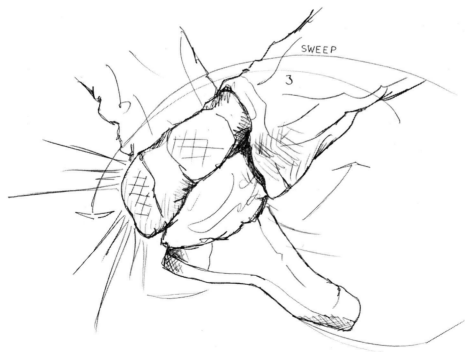

Figure 276

Action 1: As both opponents come to grips, opponent B steps forward onto opponent A's foot. When A reacts by pulling his foot back, B pulls his weapon arm back and down while simultaneously pulling up and ripping the weapon hand free, as shown in Figure 277.

Action 2: When B feels his opponent's balance shift to the right, he swings his left leg across into a sweep to topple the opponent, as seen in Figure 278.

Figure 277

Figure 278

Adding the Kicks

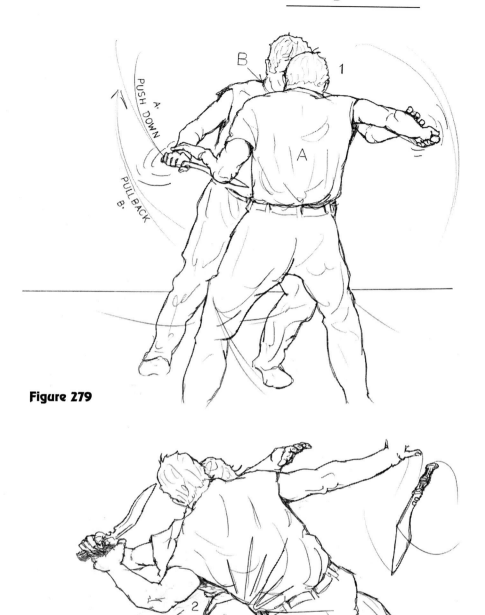

Figure 279

Figure 280

The Knee Strike

This technique is usually used inside the box against an opponent who is firmly grounded. Knee strikes are effective against targets B, C, D, or G, along with the groin and hip areas. Figure 279 through 280 illustrate how the knee strike is used in conjunction with push/pulling hand techniques to topple an opponent.

Action 1: As the opponents come to grips, B pushes both of A's arms back, as shown in Figure 279. As opponent A pushes back, B pulls his weapon arm back.

Action 2: As opponent A reacts by again pulling back, B raises his weapon arm and delivers a knee strike to the left hip, as shown in Figure 280.

Another example of the knee strike is shown in Figures 281 through 282. Here we move from medium to close range.

Action 1: Opponent A drives in, trapping B's weapon arm against his face with a two-handed block, as illustrated in Figure 281.

Action 2: Before B can disengage his weapon arm, A delivers a knee strike to the groin, as shown in Figure 282.

Note: We have only just scratched the surface of the wealth of material available on kicks and associated leg techniques. I encourage readers to not limit your study to the few techniques we have incorporated here but rather to explore a variety of methods from a variety of systems.

Figure 281

Figure 282

Training Note 16 Adding the Reverse Grip

The history of knife fighting is full of numerous examples of the knife being used in the reverse grip, where the point is down as illustrated in Figure 283. You will see this in both Asian and Western martial methods. The manuscripts of the medieval and Renaissance eras are replete with a variety of offensive and defensive techniques where the dagger is used in reverse grip as a backup weapon. While the reverse grip does not fully capitalize on the blade design of the kukri, it is worth learning if only for the possibility of your ending up holding the weapon in that position.

In terms of accessing, the kukri will come out of the sheath in the reverse grip just as quickly as the saber grip. At medium range, the reverse grip gives up some distance to the saber grip, causing the fighter to extend the shoulder or move forward to compensate, as illustrated in Figure 284. Another disadvantage is that the hand is vulnerable to being hit during the initiation of a reverse grip cut.

After a decade of working with various reverse and saber techniques, I've come to the conclusion that the reverse grip works best within the close-quarter circle we discussed earlier and illustrated in

Figure 283

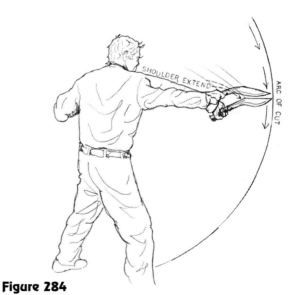

Figure 284

Figure 285. Here it is particularly effective in executing cuts upward from the low-line area, similar to the movement shown in Figure 286. It is from this aspect that we will explore the kukri in the reverse grip.

As with the saber grip, reverse grip cuts and stabs can be done with one or two hands, the latter in a power-assisted mode to overcome an opponent's blocks or pinning techniques, as illustrated in Figure 287. Those powerful upward cuts with the reverse grip are delivered in two actions, depicted in Figure 288. Step 1 involves snapping the edge out and up, as illustrated in drawing A. As the blade moves out

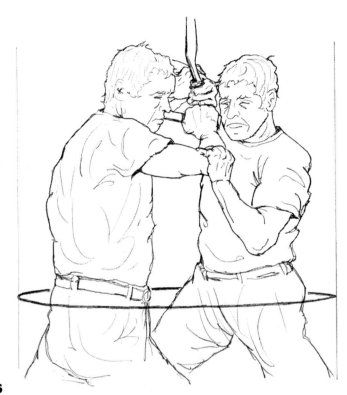

Figure 285

Figure 286

Adding the Reverse Grip

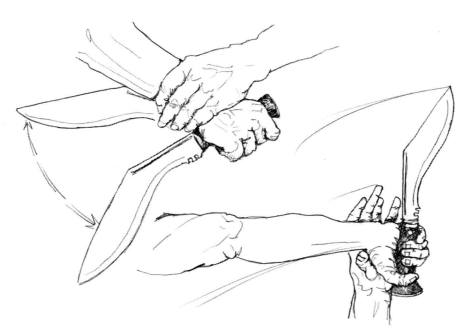

Figure 287

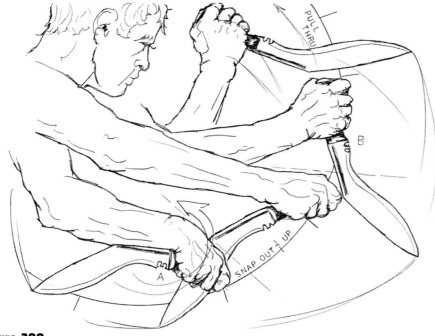

Figure 288

past the hand, the arm is extended out and up into the circular pulling action shown in drawing B.

A final point here is that the reverse grip may employ the edge out or in, as illustrated earlier in Figure 283. Remember that most kukris are not double edged and therefore with the spine forward, the techniques are somewhat limited to blocking or deflecting. Another point: the guards for the reverse grip are identical to those illustrated in Figures 24 through 26. The only difference is that the hands are rotated about 5 degrees forward, pulling the edge out and raising the hands slightly to present the blade.

WORKING THE ANGLES

Keeping those introductory thoughts in mind, let's try some application of the cutting angles we learned earlier. For clarity, we will identify the angles by the same numbers we used in the earlier chapters and review in Figure 289. The only difference is that we will start our cutting pattern at the low-line area and work our way up, as in a scenario for the close-quarter circle.

Action 1: Begin with the weak side forward in a low guard position. Execute a passing step forward with the right leg to close the distance to the opponent. Simultaneously, snap the blade forward and pull the kukri up into the arc of an angle 3 cut across the knee, thigh, and lower abdomen, as depicted in Figure 290.

Action 2: As the angle 3 cut reaches its apex, rotate the pommel down and execute an angle 2 cut, as illustrated in Figure 291.

Note: Both Action 1 and 2 should be executed as one fluid motion while stepping to your right and

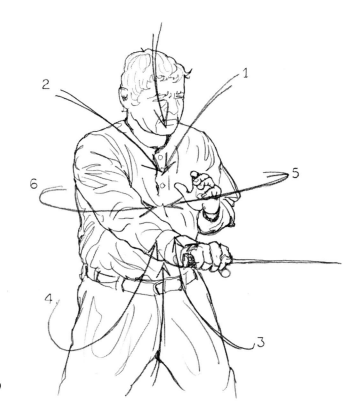

Figure 289

Figure 290

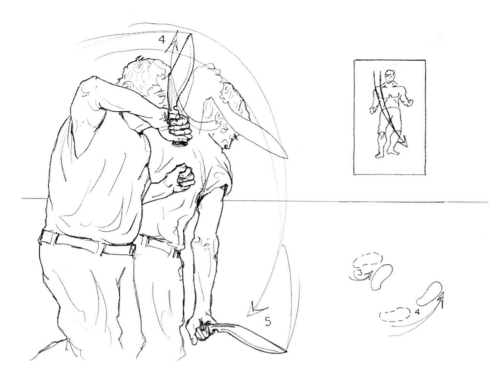

Figure 291

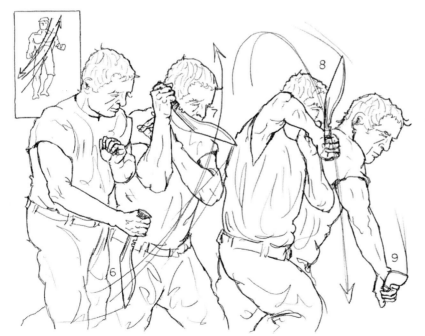

Figure 292

around your opponent to a position outside the box.

Action 3: As angle 2 reaches the bottom of its arc, flip the kukri to a pommel-up position and execute an angle 4 cut, as shown in drawings 6 and 7 of Figure 292.

Action 4: When the angle 4 reaches its apex, flip the kukri to a pommel-down position and execute an angle 1 cut, as illustrated in drawings 8 and 9 of Figure 292.

Note: Both Action 3 and 4 should be executed as one fluid motion while stepping to your right and around your opponent to a position outside the box.

Note: Practice Actions 1 through 4 as a complete sequence, moving rapidly from one to another while visualizing moving around the opponent to either the left or right outside the box. As with our earlier exercises, you first want to become proficient executing this as a solo flow sequence in front of a mirror or in the open air. Move on to performing the sequence on a heavy bag with a training knife, then on the pell with live steel.

THE CIRCULAR RELEASE

The circular release techniques we discussed for the saber grip are essentially the same as those for the reverse grip. The biggest difference is that the point is down, and angle of movement requires a bit more manipulation of the blade.

As with the saber grip, the reverse grip uses two circular release techniques. Figure 293 illustrates the inside release. The action starts by rotating the pommel around and under the opponent's arm. As the pommel rises to the inside, rotate the point up and over and bring the blade down on the outside of the opponent's arm, as shown in Figure 294. When the blade is in that position, turn the wrist out and deliver a slight pull back. Immediately on feeling the opponent resist, rip the kukri out and into a high or middle line cut.

Figure 293

Figure 294

Adding the Reverse Grip

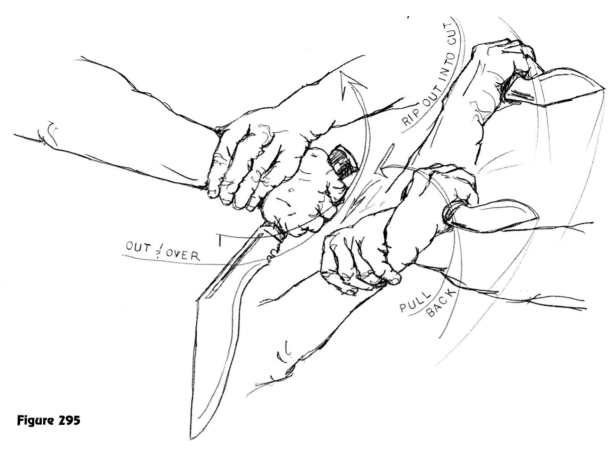

OUT & OVER

RIP OUT INTO CUT

PULL BACK

Figure 295

One version of the outside circular release is depicted in Figure 295. This technique begins by rotating the pommel around and to the outside of the opponent's gripping arm. As the pommel comes up over the wrist, exert pressure on the opponent's wrist joint. From here, rip the kukri out and around into a circular arc that terminates in a slash to a high-line target. Another version involves continuing to rotate the blade around into a position on the inside of the opponent's arm, similar to what is shown in Figure 294. From there, the execution is basically the same.

Note: Practice these releases with a training partner, just as we did earlier with the saber grip, until you are comfortable.

THE CLOSE-QUARTER ROTATION

When executing a circular release, the size and strength of your opponent may make it necessary to add another direction of force to make the escape effective. The following exercise uses the torque generated by twisting the hips and torso to complement either inside or outside circular releases while in the reverse grip.

Action 1: Begin by executing an outside circular release (not shown). As the release is completed, pivot to the left and violently rip the kukri upward into an ascending arc, as shown in Figure 296.

Action 2: Execute an inside circular release followed by a pivot to the right, as shown in Figure 297. Immediately execute a circular arc upward to rip the kukri out of the opponent's hand.

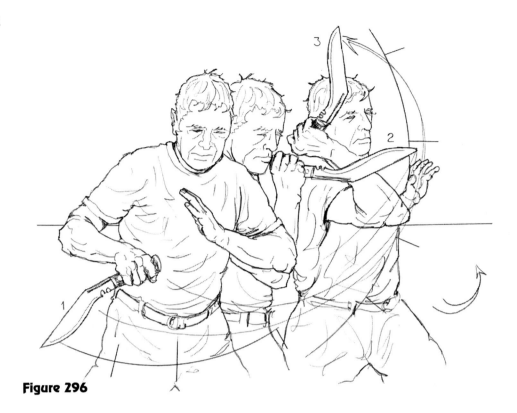

Figure 296

Figure 297

Adding the Reverse Grip

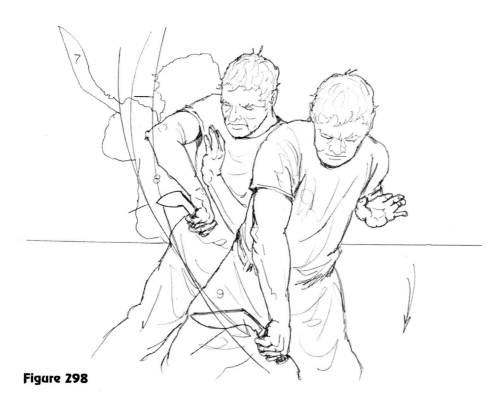

Figure 298

Figure 299

Action 3: Execute a high-line, inside circular release while rotating the hips to your right. Follow with a violent downward arc illustrated in Figure 298.

Action 4: Execute a low-line, outside circular release followed by a rip away up into a vertical arc, as illustrated in Figure 299. The hips may be rotated to the left or right.

Note: Practice Actions 1 through 4 as a complete sequence, moving rapidly from one action to another while visualizing moving around the opponent to either the left or right outside the box. As with our earlier exercises, you will want to first become proficient executing this as a solo flow sequence in front of a mirror or in the open air. Move on to performing the sequence on a heavy bag with a training knife, then later on the pell with live steel. As proficiency increases, move on to executing the technique with a resisting training partner.

USING BRIDGING TECHNIQUES

A close cousin to the circular release is a technique called "bridging." Basically, this is a block followed by a circular release, and it is well-suited to the reverse grip. Bridges can be performed against incoming attacks in the high and middle-line areas, both inside and outside the box. For lack of a better word, let's identify them as an inside or outside bridge.

Inside Bridge

Figure 300 illustrates the flow for the inside bridge. This begins by first effecting a point-down vertical block as shown in drawing 1. Immediately on impact, rotate the blade around, under, and over the opponent's blade arm as depicted in drawing 2 and ending in a position shown in drawing 3. From this position, one can either execute a circular cut or stab, as shown in drawing 4. It is important to note that it may be necessary to use your opposite hand to stabilize his weapon arm. As with all bridges, this one must be executed quickly and in one smooth, flowing motion. If your opponent moves to disengage, you might not be able to pull the bridge off!

Figure 300

Figure 301

Adding the Reverse Grip

Figure 302

Figures 301 and 302 illustrate the practical application of this bridge.

The Outside Bridge

The flow for the outside bridge is depicted in Figure 303. As before, this begins with a point-down vertical block on the opponent's incoming weapon arm, as depicted in drawing 1. On impact, rotate the blade to the outside as shown in drawing 2. Follow immediately with either a stab or cut similar to drawing 3. The application for this bridge is illustrated in Figures 304 through 306.

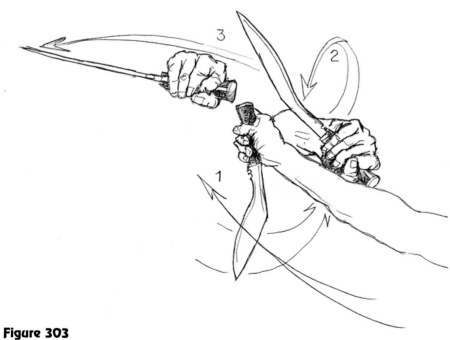

Figure 303

The Fighting Kukri

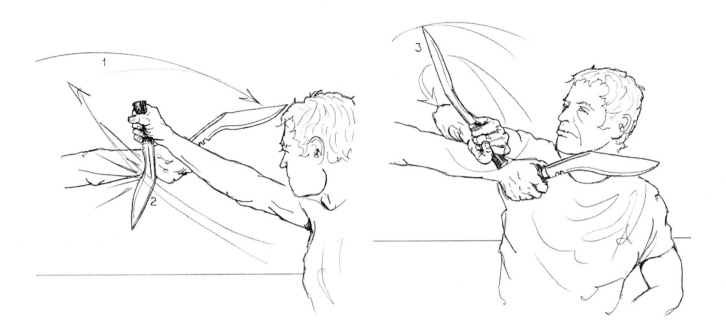

Figure 304

Figure 305

Figure 306

Adding the Reverse Grip

A CLASSIC EXAMPLE

Figure 307 shows one of the classic examples of employment of the reverse grip. We'll include more in the engagement scenarios. The action begins with an imaginary opponent executing an angle 1 cut to the left side of our fighter's neck. Immediately, the fighter grabs and torques the opponent's weapon wrist to the left while sliding into close quarters and accessing his kukri from a right-side carry. As the kukri clears the sheath, he executes an angle 3 upward cut to the opponent's weapon arm. Figures 308 and 309 depict the practical application of this technique.

Figure 307

Figure 308

The Fighting Kukri

Figure 309

Training Note 17 From Flat on Your Back

I never felt that ground training was ever addressed sufficiently in any of the training manuals I have written. Yes, there are a lot of great publications that cover ground fighting, but these are mostly from an empty hand perspective, or what has been termed "mixed martial arts." Now don't get me wrong: there is a lot of valuable information in these publications, especially those that deal with disarming a knife-welding opponent from a ground position. It is just that the coverage is a bit light. I encourage you to round out your study of weapons by working with a variety of grappling material and adapting it to your personal needs.

My friend and mentor, W. Hoch Hochheim, has produced a remarkably useful group of videos that cover this subject in a simple, practical manner. His set of ground fighting exercises with and against the knife are applicable to the modern world and a variety of weapons. If some of the material in this training note looks familiar, it is because it came from the time when I studied with the man. Thanks, Hoch!

THE REALITY OF THE GROUND FIGHT

Throughout history, many martial masters have warned against the dangers of going to ground with an opponent. The medieval Italian master Fiore dei Liberi mentions that it is preferred to topple an armed opponent rather than wrestle with him. All that said, the bottom line is that many of the grappling techniques require some modification when both you and

your opponent are armed. It is from that perspective that we will approach this training note.

There are really four basic causes for ending up on the ground: tripping over your own feet, tripping over some object during your movement, being toppled by the opponent, or when the opponent closes, grapples, and takes you to the ground. It is generally safe to say that in most circumstances, you will end up either on your back or side, not unlike what's depicted in Figure 310.

Figure 311 illustrates the actions that your armed opponent must take to accomplish this, whether by topple or grapple. First, he must secure your weapon arm to deal with the steel. In our example, he has chosen to close and seize the weapon arm. Simultaneously, he must disrupt by striking a vulnerable area. In our scenario, he drives his head or shoulder into the opponent's chin or chest while reaching down to hook the leg with the pommel of his knife. The third step involves unbalancing the opponent, such as continuing to push forward while pulling the opponent's lead leg off the ground.

Once these actions have occurred, the fighter may choose to continue the attack from a standing position or follow his opponent to the ground. From the standing position, he might use his feet to pin the weapon arm, as illustrated in Figure 312. If the opponent drops down on you, he will often use his knee and empty hand to pin the weapon and head momentarily prior to delivering a cut, as shown in Figure 313.

The Fighting Kukri

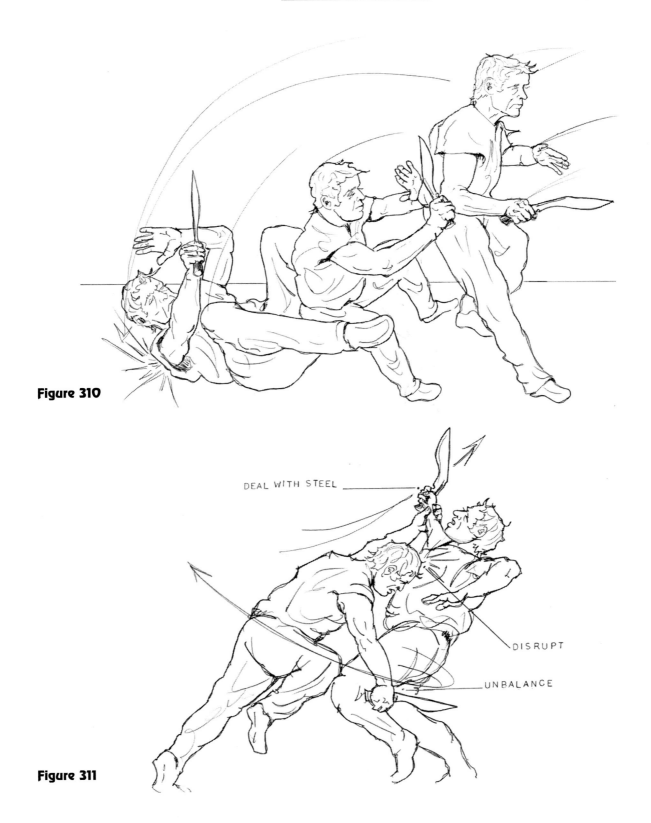

Figure 310

DEAL WITH STEEL

DISRUPT

UNBALANCE

Figure 311

From Flat on Your Back

Figure 312

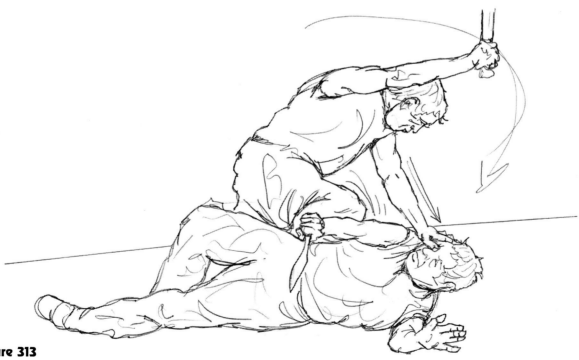

Figure 313

We will examine the counters to these later, but for now here are some facts about fighting flat on your back. First of all, if your opponent attempts to continue the attack from a standing position, it is not necessarily the end of the world for you. When you are on your back as illustrated in Figure 314, your opponent must step close to you in order to access any target area. This makes him vulnerable to low- and middle-line attacks that can be delivered from a prone or sitting position. He must bend forward or squat to attack you, whereas you have all four limbs that can be employed without becoming unbalanced. In this situation, the opponent has only one defensive triangle that can be brought up to assist in attack and defense. From the prone and sitting position, you can bring the legs into play as another defensive triangle and as means of tripping or kicking, as shown in Figure 314.

Figures 315 and 316 illustrate the two defensive triangles that can be employed from the prone and sitting position to attack and defend a standing opponent. Let's take a moment and explore some of the movement options when fighting from the prone position.

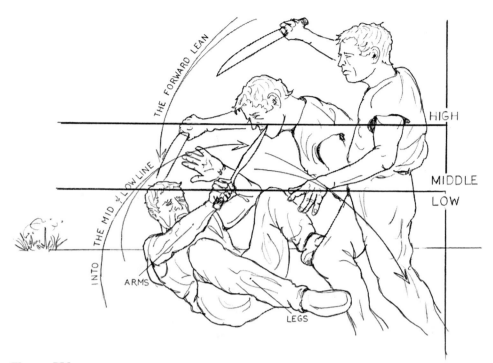

Figure 314

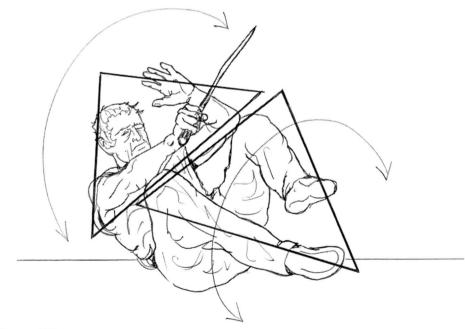

Figure 315

ASPECTS OF LEFT AND RIGHT MOVE-MENT FROM THE PRONE POSITION

Figure 316

As seen in Figure 315, the defensive triangles formed by the arms and legs can be maintained in almost any direction from the ground. While the fore-arms and shins do not pro-vide total protection against well-aimed full-force blows, they offer the options to deflect or launch attacks at the opponent's middle and low-line area.

Action 1: Take up a prone position with the arms and legs forming the defensive triangle we addressed above. While maintaining a two-handed middle guard position, visualize an opponent mov-ing in to your left. Swing the right knee over to the left and pull the left knee back and under while turn-ing the torso to the left. Make sure to maintain the guard as you turn and use the kukri to block or cut at any incoming attack, as illustrated in Figure 317.

Figure 317

Action 2: Visualize an opponent moving in from your right and immediately repeat Action 1 by rolling to the right, as illustrated in Figure 318.

Note: Repeat Actions 1 and 2 until you get comfortable swinging one knee over and pulling the opposite leg under. Practice until it becomes natural.

Action 3: In this sequence, we will add the short and long strike cuts as you roll through the two defensive triangles, similar to that shown in Figure 319. Begin by rolling left and executing the strike, then to the right and repeating the cut. As you experiment with both long and short strikes, you will notice that it is difficult to execute the traditional cutting pattern we used when standing upright. You will also find that the long strikes do not have the momentum they normally would.

That said, here is a short strike technique that works well from the prone position. Using Figure 319 as a guide, roll to the right and execute an angle 5 short strike cut. On completion, flip the blade over and roll back to the left, executing an angle 6 short strike cut.

Action 4: Experiment moving from the prone to the sitting position. You will

Figure 318

Figure 319

Figure 320

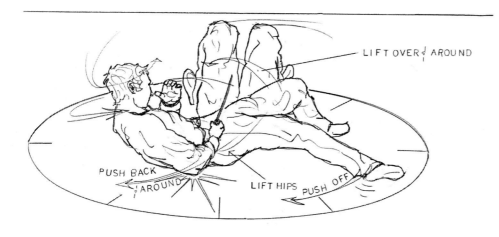

Figure 321

see that the long strike's effectiveness increases. Continue to practice this as you move up to one knee. Notice that from here you can put a little hip action into the long strike to improve the momentum.

While movement in the prone position is limited, it is certainly not out of the question. Yes, it requires more practice, but there are options that can open the door to some really good opportunities for attack and counterattack.

In the previous training exercise, we worked with rolling both left and right to counter a threat to those sides. Another option involves spinning around on one's butt and small of the back, as illustrated in Figure 320. During these spins, the arms form that defensive triangle we discussed earlier, and the legs are lifted up and pointed toward the opponent, as seen in drawing A. This method of circling with the opponent's movement is accomplished by pushing off on the elbow, lifting the hips, and pushing off with the foot while lifting the legs up, over, and around, as visualized in Figure 321. As I said, this technique requires a bit of practice to master, and you will definitely need a strong core muscle group to be able to sustain it. Sit-ups, hip rolls, and leg lifts are good training exercises for this. Let's look at a couple of practical applications for the rolling and spin techniques from the prone position.

Scenario 1

Visualize your opponent stepping into your right side with his left leg, as illustrated in Figure 322. Suddenly, he draws his right leg back and into a kick. Recognizing the cue, you roll to your right and deliver a cut to his knee. Simultaneously, disrupt the incoming kick by delivering a toe kick to his groin.

Scenario 2

Visualize an opponent stepping into your left side with his left leg leading. Using the spin technique we just discussed, spin to your left, bringing your leg

Figure 322

Figure 323

From Flat on Your Back

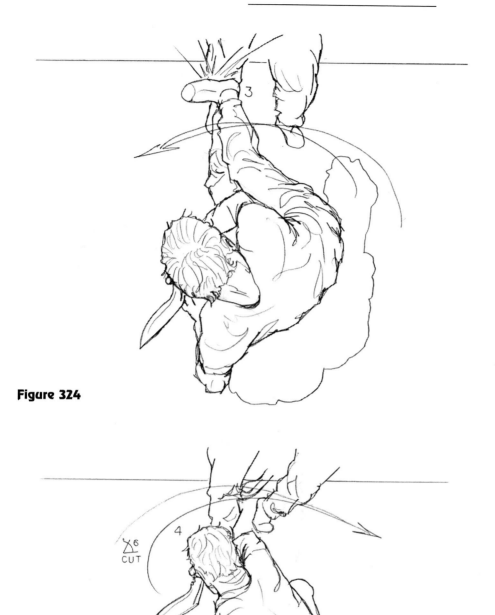

Figure 324

Figure 325

around till you face him in the position in Figure 323. Before he can lean forward to strike you, hook your left foot behind his leg and roll to your left, moving up into a forearm-supported position and delivering a kick to his knee, as illustrated in Figure 324. Do not pull the kicking leg back too fast; rather, keep it on the knee and continue to hook and push until the opponent goes down. Should this not be successful, continue to move up into a hand-supported sitting position and deliver an angle 6 cut to the opponent's knee as indicated in Figure 325.

Note: Practice these two scenarios with a training partner at slow and medium speed. Be especially careful not to damage your partner's knee while practicing the second scenario.

ASPECTS OF LEFT AND RIGHT MOVEMENT FROM THE SEATED POSITION

The aspects of fighting from the seated position might be considered by some as just another method of bouncing around on your butt. As you can see from Figure 326, the attack angles are a bit awkward, often requiring one to move to the left or right to complete the cut. Now, I am not saying not to practice from the seated position but rather to think of it as a transition point from the prone to the kneeling position, as shown in Figure 327. As you look at this drawing, note that the fighter steps over the opposite leg and continues to turn onto one knee. Take a moment and practice this. Note how this movement takes you out to the side and away from any incoming attack while simultaneously swinging the blade arm through either a deflection or cut that finishes in a kneeling position. When you are comfortable with this action, expand the technique by taking it through the exercise set illustrated in Figures 328 through 330.

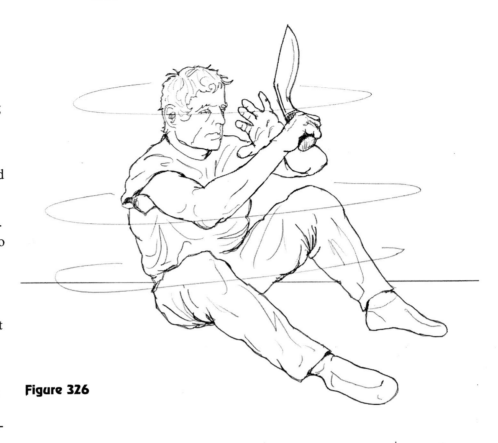

Figure 326

Figure 327

From Flat on Your Back

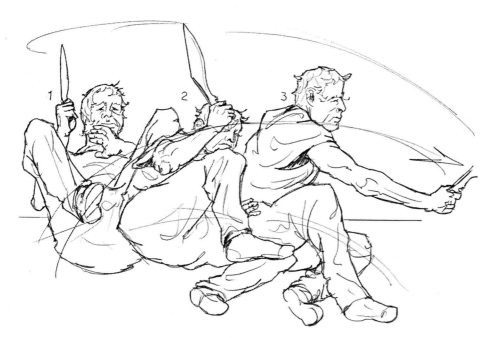

Figure 328

Action 1: Beginning in a prone position, visualize an opponent attacking from the left. Roll to your left, step over, and deliver a cut to the opponent's lead leg or his incoming weapon hand, as illustrated in Figure 328.

Action 2: Drop back into the seated position depicted in Figure 329 and deliver an angle 6 cut back at an opponent attacking from the right.

Figure 329

Action 3: Visualize an opponent delivering a kick to your midsection. Roll back into a prone position, then to your right, stepping over and back up into the seated position to deliver a countercut as illustrated in Figure 330.

Note: Practice this exercise as part of your warm-up immediately after working the upright stepping patterns we discussed earlier. After you have mastered the exercise, have a training partner deliver simulated attacks, as illustrated in Figures 331 and 332. As he steps in and delivers a cut, counter with a disruption cut to the hand, then the hook and push technique we addressed in Figures 323 through 325.

At this point we have only touched the surface of the multitude of ground fighting methods that can accommodate the kukri. It is recommended that you research various other disciplines and find the ones that work best for you. Here are a couple of commonly used scenarios that you can practice.

Figure 330

Figure 331

From Flat on Your Back

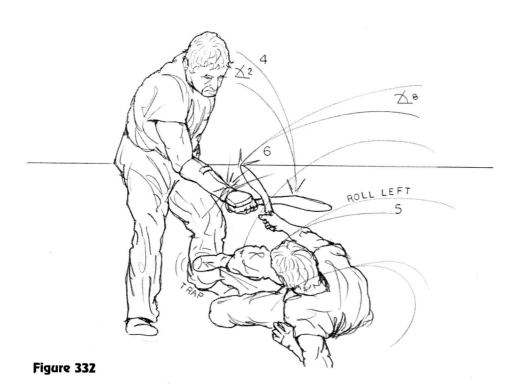

Figure 332

Scenario 1

Visualize an opponent kneeling on your right side and grasping your weapon hand. As he draws back to deliver a cut, seize the wrist of the weapon arm and roll to the right, using the forearm as a lever on that arm. Continue to roll to the right, slamming the opponent onto the ground and delivering a cut to a vital area, as illustrated in Figure 333.

Figures 334 through 336 illustrate this application. Note that a circular release can also be used in association with the forearm lever.

Figure 333

The Fighting Kukri

Figure 334

Figure 335

Figure 336

From Flat on Your Back

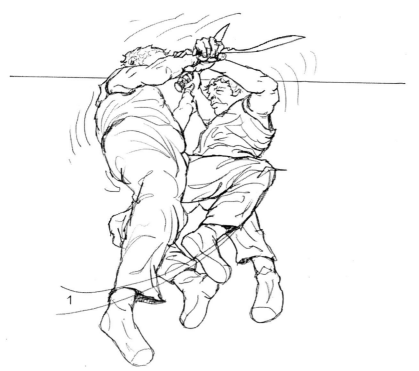

Figure 337

Scenario 2

Visualize you and your opponent hand-on-hand, with you in a prone position after going to the ground. You are on your left side, as illustrated in Figure 337. As soon as you hit the ground, bring your left knee up onto your opponent's weapon hand, as illustrated in Figure 338. As you pin his arm, move up into a semi-seated position and deliver a kick to his arm, as shown in Figure 339. Continue to move up into a seated position while simultaneously delivering the angle 7 cut shown in Figure 340.

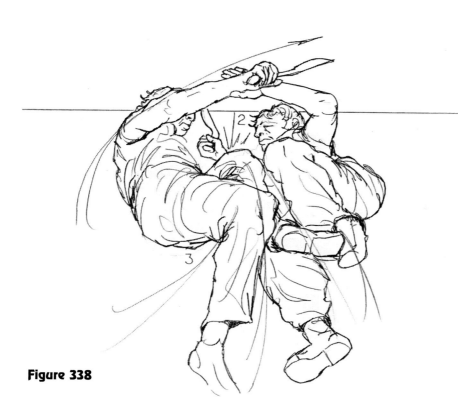

Figure 338

The Fighting Kukri

Figure 339

Figure 340

BOOK 3 Portfolio of Engagement Scenarios

The following 15 engagement scenarios depict practical application of the techniques I covered throughout the text. These are lifted directly from my sketchbook and field notes from the past 10 years. In some you will see a variety of knives other than the kukri, but I included them for their ease of application to that weapon. Since most of these techniques pretty much stand alone in terms of clarity, there is no explanatory text. In some cases, the techniques will be presented with a solo set and application sequence. I see these being used as a guide to training in three aspects:

Aspect 1: Practice the scenario as a solo set in the open air; then duplicate it on a heavy bag.

Aspect 2: Practice the scenario with a training partner, moving from slow, medium, to fast speed while each partner rotates through the various roles.

Aspect 3: Practice as controlled sparring with padded weapons and full protective equipment. Remember that with this training, each partner has to stick to his part in the scenario. This is not free sparring.

Engagement Set 1

Engagement Set 1

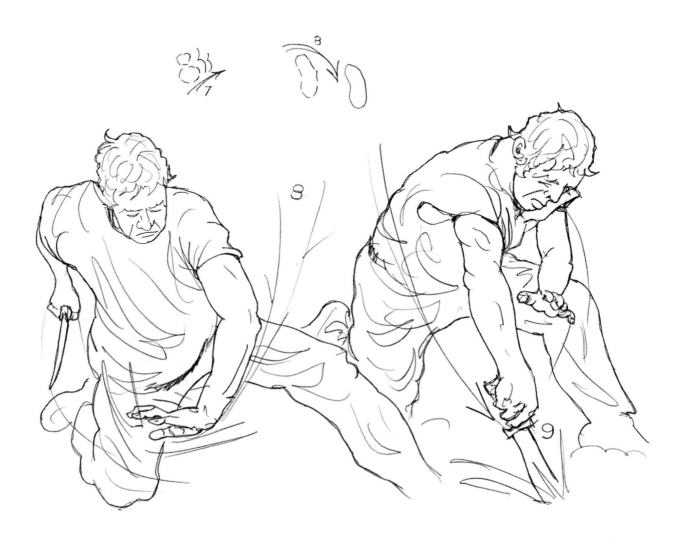

Engagement Set 2

The Fighting Kukri

Engagement Set 2

Engagement Set 3

Engagement Set 3

APPLICATION

245

The Fighting Kukri

Engagement Set 3

The Fighting Kukri

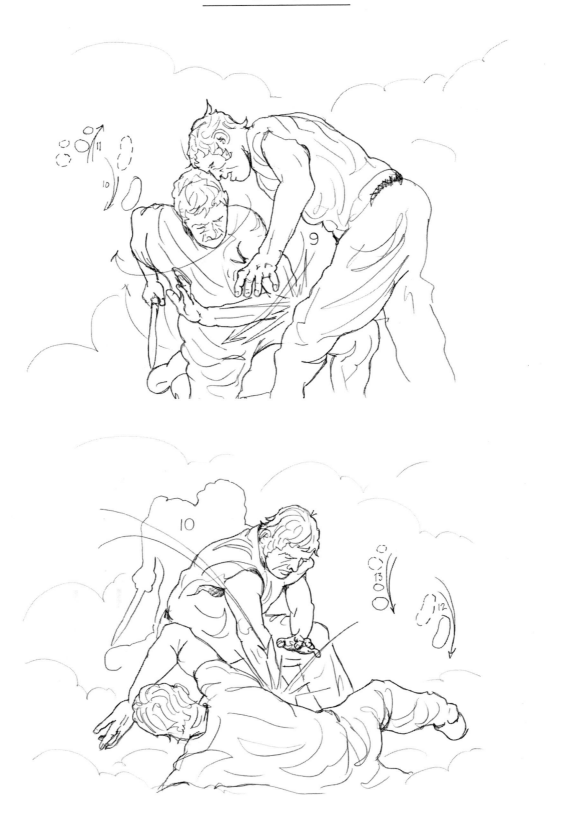

Engagement Set 4

The Fighting Kukri

APPLICATION

Engagement Set 4

The Fighting Kukri

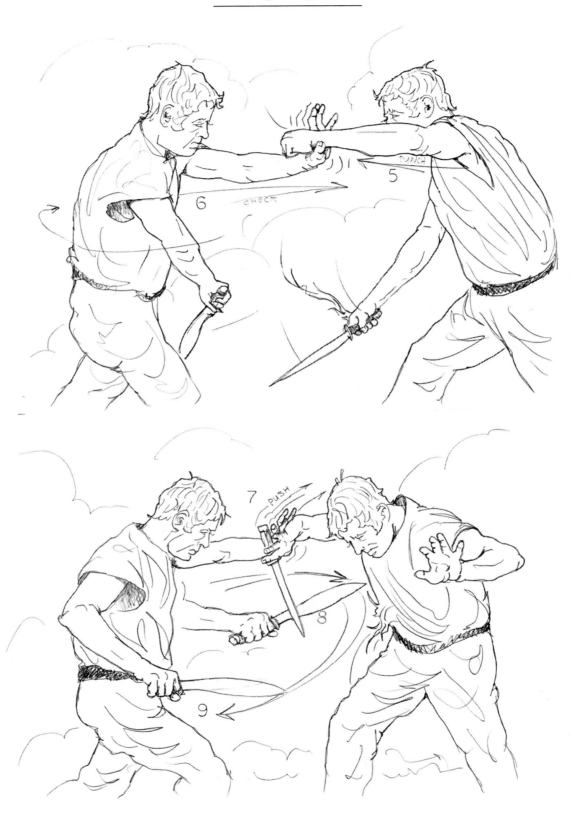

Engagement Set 5

Engagement Set 5

APPLICATION

GRAB & PULL

STOP!

The Fighting Kukri

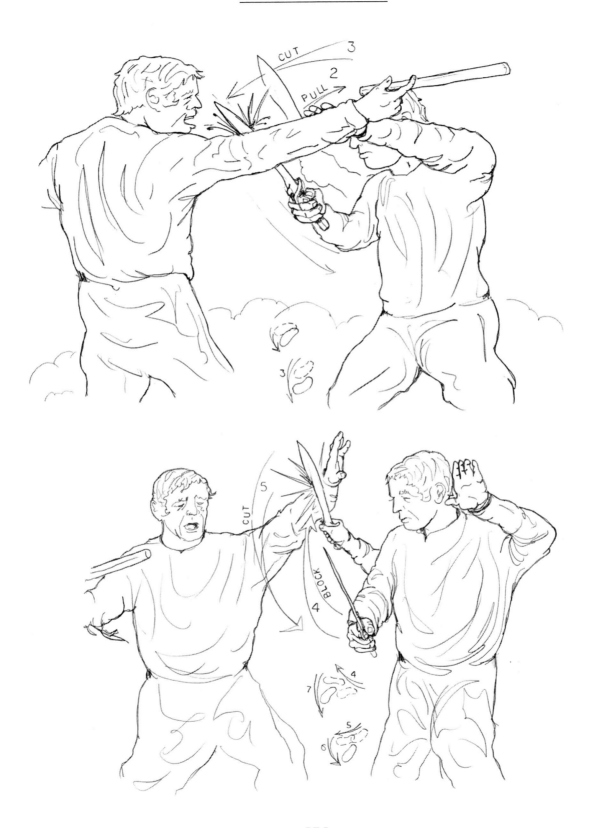

Engagement Set 5

The Fighting Kukri

Engagement Set 6

The Fighting Kukri

THRUST BACK

Engagement Set 7

Engagement Set 7

Engagement Set 8

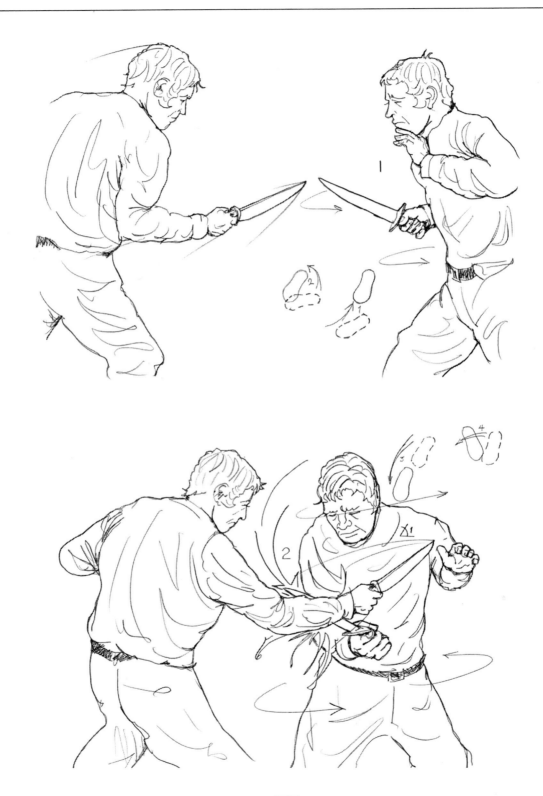

Engagement Set 8

Engagement Set 9

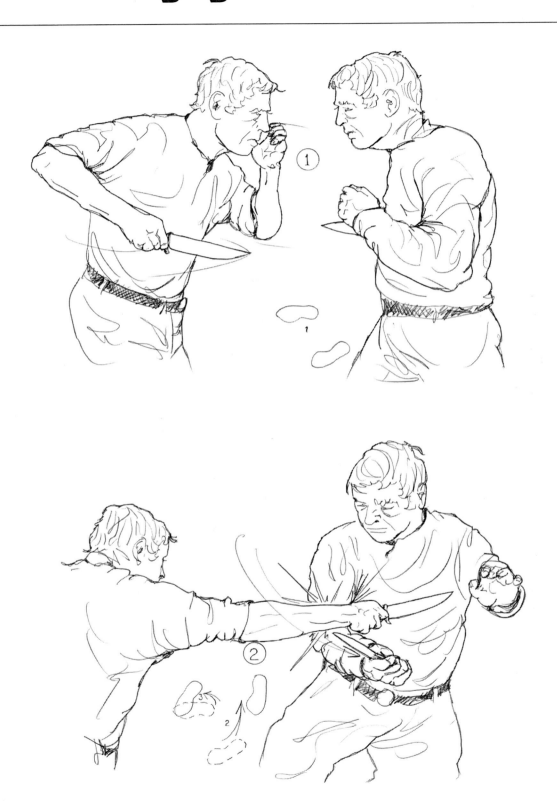

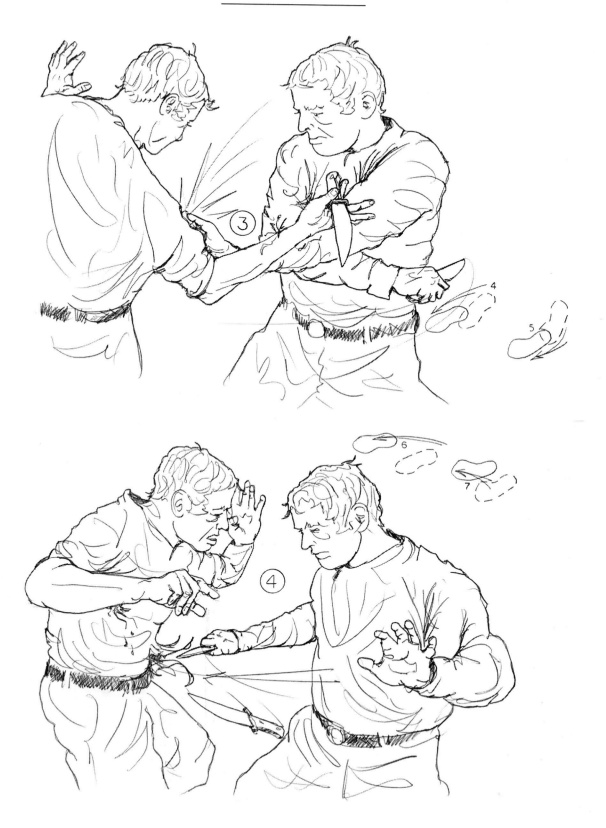

The Fighting Kukri

Engagement Set 10

GRAB

The Fighting Kukri

Engagement Set 11

The Fighting Kukri

Engagement Set 12

Engagement Set 12

Engagement Set 13

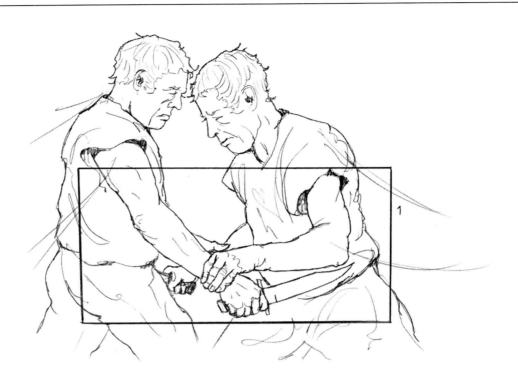

The Fighting Kukri

Engagement Set 14

The Fighting Kukri

Engagement Set 15

Engagement Set 15

The Fighting Kukri

The Fighting Kukri

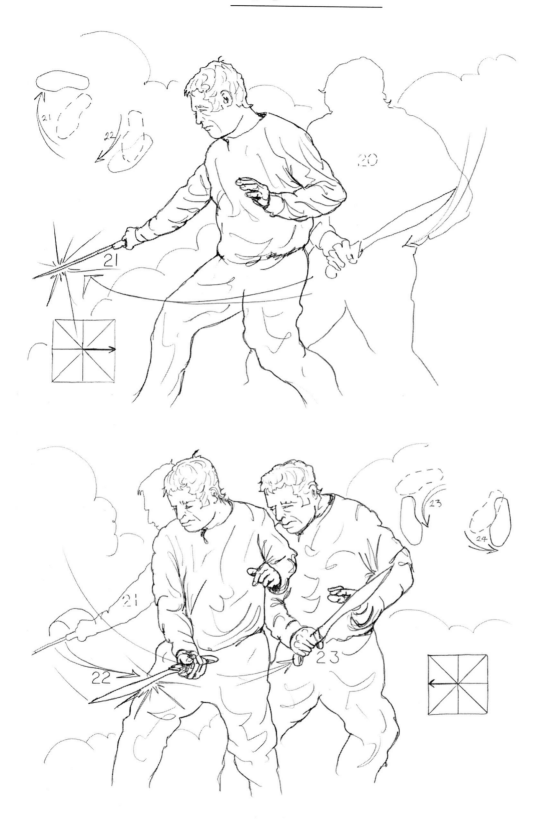

The Fighting Kukri

The Fighting Kukri

290

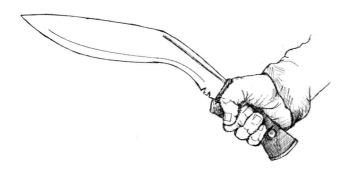

Special Thanks and Closing Thoughts

Special thanks to the staff and craftsmen of Khukuri House (www.khukurihouseonline.com) for providing me with the beautiful and functional *aitihasik* kukri. I have come to think of this historic design as an old friend, answering my functional design questions that always seem to pop up during the writing of any text.

Every good knife needs a good training version. I want to thank John Stanley of TAK knives (www.takknife.com) for providing me with the excellent carbon fiber version of the aitihasik.

Conclusion? There is no conclusion! Rather, what I hope is that this is just the beginning for many of you who study edged weapons. It is my wish that I have been somewhat helpful to you in your martial journeys. I know it is smart to "never say never," but in all probability this will be my last text in this weapons training series. As I move into the later phases of life, I've concluded it is time to go back and pursue some of those artistic things I did when I was younger. I want to personally thank my publisher, Paladin Press, and all of you for believing in me and taking the time to read my books. I will close with this quote from the late Joseph Campbell:

"When you follow your bliss, doors will open where you would not have thought . . ."

Good luck,
Dwight

Selected References

Amberger, J. Christoph. *The Secret History of the Sword*. New York: Multi-Media Books, 1999.

Bagwell, Bill. *Bowies, Big Knives and the Best of Battle Blades*. Boulder, CO: Paladin Press, 2000.

Burton, Richard F. *The Book of the Sword*. London: Chatto & Windus, 1884; (reprint edition) Mineola, NY: Dover Publications, 1987.

Cassidy, William L. *The Complete Book of Knife Fighting*. Boulder, CO: Paladin Press, 1975.

Draeger, Donn F., and Robert W. Smith. *Comprehensive Asian Fighting Arts*. Tokyo: Kodansha International Ltd., 1969; (reprint edition) New York: Kodansha USA, 1981.

Dukes, Terence (trans.). *The Bodhisattva Warriors*. York Beach, ME: Samuel Weiser, Inc., 1994.

Grant, R. G. *Warrior: A Visual History of the Fighting Man*. London: DK Publishing, 2007.

Grosz, Christopher, and Michael Janich. *Contemporary Knife Targeting*. Boulder, CO: Paladin Press, 2006.

Hochheim, Hoch. *Knife Fighting Encyclopedia, Vol. I*. Allen, TX: Lauric Press, 1996.

————. *Military Knife Combat*. Allen, TX: Lauric Press, 1999.

Martinez, Rafael. *Rome's Enemies: Spanish Armies*. Oxford: Osprey Publishing, 1986.

Masters, John. *Bugles and a Tiger: My Life in the Gurkhas*. New York: Viking Press, 1956; (reprint edition) New York: Sterling Publishing, 2002.

McLemore, Dwight C. *Advanced Bowie Techniques*. Boulder, CO: Paladin Press, 2006.

————. *Bowie and Big-Knife Fighting System*. Boulder, CO: Paladin Press, 2003.

————. *The Fighting Sword*. Boulder, CO: Paladin Press, 2008.

————. *The Fighting Tomahawk*. Boulder, CO: Paladin Press, 2004.

————. *The Fighting Tomahawk, Vol. II*. Boulder, CO: Paladin Press, 2010.

Peterson, Peter (trans). *Dhanurveda* (on "The Science of the Horn Bow"), Bombay, 1888; (reprint edition) Chakravarti, B. (trans.). Kolkata: ATARN, 2001.

Sanz-Quesada, Fernando. *Machaira, Kopis, Falcata*. Madrid: Homenaje a Francisco Torrent, 1994.

Sato, Hiroaki (trans). *The Sword and the Mind*. New York: Overlook Press, 1988.

Sekunda, Nicholas. *The Army of Alexander the Great*. Oxford: Osprey Publishing, 1984.

Simonet, Joseph, and Michael Janich. *Silat Concepts, Form and Function*. Boulder, CO: Paladin Press, 2004.

Tedeschi, Marc. *Essential Anatomy for Healing and Martial Arts*. Boston: Weatherhill, 2000.

Warry, John. *Warfare in the Classical World*. Norman, OK: University of Oklahoma Press, 1995.

Wilcox, Peter. *Rome's Enemies: Gallic and British Celts*. Oxford: Osprey Publishing, 1985.

Wise, Terence. *Armies of the Carthaginian Wars, 265–146 BC*. Oxford: Osprey Publishing, 1982.

Zarrilli, Phillip B. "Actualizing Power(s) and Crafting a Self in Kalarippayattu," *Journal of Asian Martial Arts*: Vol. 3, No. 3, 1994.

COASTAL BIRDS

Richard Allen

ISBN 978-0-9926877-1-7
Jardine Press Ltd 2014
www.jardinepress.co.uk

limited edition prints of the images
in this book are available from the author

for Sally

Contents

Introduction

Introduction

Coming originally from land-locked Berkshire, I never tire of walking my dog Buster along the Colne estuary and observing the ever changing scene of birds, tides and weather. There is always something interesting going on, pairs of Oystercatchers squabbling over territory, a Marsh Harrier drifting along the seawall, or a seal crunching on a Dab. The bird population of the estuary is also constantly changing, as I write this the Black-tailed Godwits are about to leave for their Icelandic nesting grounds, while the Lapwings and Golden Plover that crowded the mud in winter are already on the meadows and moors of eastern Europe.

"Coastal Birds" is a collection of linocuts inspired by the birds that regularly haunt and bring to life my *local patch of shoreline. I am particularly attracted to birds with bold dynamic plumage such as Lapwings, Shelduck and Oystercatchers, and the patterns found in their habitat of water, mud and sky. The Avocet is a special favourite, one that I spend many hours sketching, a rare bird in my early birdwatching days it is now a frequent sight on this east coast estuary.*

Richard Allen

Wivenhoe
April 2014

Dabchick

Also called the Little Grebe, these small dumpy birds arrive on the estuary in winter, where they dive for small fish and shrimps in creeks and inlets.

They are mostly buff and dark brown coloured, and appear very buoyant in the water and have a tendency to fluff up their rear end.

In summer Dabchicks have a rich chestnut patch on cheeks and neck and a yellow base to the bill. Moving onto fresh water to breed they frequent small ponds and ditches building a floating nest from where they hatch three or four stripy necked chicks.

Cormorant

A large black bird perched on a buoy or groyne with out-stretched wings will be a Cormorant. These prehistoric looking birds lack the water-proofing abilities of other seabirds and so must hang out their plumage to dry after a fishing sortie. A closer look will show a glossy blue shine to feathers and in the spring a white thigh patch.

Eels and small flatfish are a favourite food in coastal waters, but they are partial any fish they can catch. In the water they look serpentine with a long neck and a smooth supple diving action.

Usually a solitary fisher they will occasionally flock together to herd shoals of sprats into shallow water to catch more easily.

Little Egret

Once a great rarity there has been a spectacular increase in the numbers of Little Egrets in recent years and it is now a common sight on our estuaries, even nesting amongst herons in their tree top colonies.

An elegant small, white heron with black legs and yellow feet, in spring they sport stylish plumes from head and breast. These were its down fall in the past as the plumes, or "aigrettes", were in high demand to adorn Victorian ladies hats.

Now with full protection they can be found stalking along narrow creeks and pools on the hunt for small fish and shrimps. They will often defend a good fishing spot, chasing off other egrets with a loud guttural croak, most unbefitting such an elegant bird.

Grey Heron

Stalking the shallow edges of creeks and marshes the Grey Heron hunts for eels, dabs and other fish especially at dawn and dusk. Taking flight with a loud "kwark" on broad powerful wings, the long serpentine neck is tucked in to the chest and the large feet trail behind.

Surprisingly for such a large bird they nest in colonies in tree-tops, building a large nest of twigs in early spring.

Brent Goose

A small dark goose that will form large dense flocks in winter which are a constant source of muttering and squabbles, although there are always a few amongst the flock on "look-out" for any danger.

The head, neck and breast is a dusky black colour with a white neck patch, the body grey with pale edging, and a white rear end.

Brent Geese nest on the arctic tundra east of the Ural Mountains amongst Arctic Foxes and Snowy Owls. In the autumn they travel SW via the Baltic with the vanguard arriving on our coast in late September with the majority arriving in October.

On arrival they feed on eel grass before moving on to graze pastures and winter wheat to build themselves up for the return north in spring.

6

Teal

Our smallest duck and a common winter visitor to muddy estuary shorelines.

The male has a chestnut head with a teal green blaze through the eye and a grey body with a horizontal white slash across the wings. The female is small and dainty, light brown with darker streaks and mottled patterning.

In late winter small groups of drakes can be seen courting females, they swim in tight circles, raising their crowns and calling a soft whistling "whoo", hoping to impress the ducks.

7

Shelduck

A handsome large duck, black and white at a distance, but a closer look reveals a green head, lipstick-pink bill, a chestnut breast band and a sulphurous yellow under tail.

Males are larger than females, and in spring are very protective of their mate as she searches for a suitable nest hole, often a rabbit burrow, to lay her eggs. Once hatched the cute black and white ducklings are led to the sea and often left in a crèche of several broods watched over by a couple of "aunties".

In winter they flock together on muddy estuaries, sieving the silt with their bills to extract their favourite food, a tiny snail called hydrobia.

8

Marsh Harrier

This impressively large bird of prey is now a common sight along coasts and estuaries, but in the early 1970s the population was down to a single nesting pair. A steady increase in numbers (after a ban on poisoning organochloride pesticides) means they can now be seen all year round quartering fields and reedbeds on broad wings held raised up in a shallow V.

Females and immature birds are largely dark brown with rich cream coloured crowns and patches on the forewing. Males are smaller and have black wing tips, pale grey panels in the wings, and a buffy-rufous body.

Avocet

Once a rare breeding bird its population has increased dramatically and it is now a regular sight on east coast estuaries. In winter large flocks form and make a spectacular sight with their flickering black and white patterns.

The only wader to have an upturned bill, it uses this to sieve small shrimps and worms from the mud's surface with a side to side swish of the head.

The call is a ringing "kloot" mostly given in flight when the long pale blue-grey legs can also be seen.

10

Oystercatcher

This is a very distinctive large black and white wader with a sturdy orange bill and pale pink legs. Feeding on shellfish they use their strong bill to smash into or prize open cockles and mussels, although they will also probe the mud for worms.

A noisy bird, especially in the spring when pairs are establishing territories, they will "pipe" loudly in unison to try and warn off rivals. At other times of the year they are very communal and roost at high tide in large dense flocks.

11

Lapwing

A characterful plover, black and white with a blue-green sheen and an often windblown crest.

A once common farmland nesting bird, it is now mainly a winter visitor. Large flocks roost on the estuary mud, especially if cold weather on the near continent forces them to flee the frozen ground.

They often feed at night, using their large eyes to find worms out on the moonlit fields. Their "pee-wit" call, an old country name for lapwings, can be heard at dusk in winter as they fly out to forage in surrounding fields.

Curlew

Our largest wader has a long down-curved bill, long grey legs and brown plumage marked with creamy streaks and crescents. Its name comes from the distinctive and mournful call, "coo-lee", commonly heard around estuaries in winter, but also echoing across its lonely moorland nesting grounds.

Generally solitary, but also forming small scattered flocks, their food of choice is the lug-worm, using their long bills to extract the worms from their U-shaped burrows. Curlews will also feed in damp meadows probing amongst the tussocks for earthworms.

13

Black-tailed Godwit

With a long straight, pink-based bill and long black legs this is an elegant wader, particularly in its rich russet and gold breeding plumage.

Leaving our estuaries in April for its Icelandic nesting grounds it returns in late summer in a drabber grey brown winter garb.

A very distinctive bird in flight sporting a broad white wing bar that distinguishes it from the very similar Bar-tailed Godwit.

The origins of the name Godwit are lost in the depths of time, but are thought to come from its "whickering" call.

14

Redshank

A medium sized grey brown wader with distinctive bright orange legs and a red base to the straight bill.

A few pairs nest each year on the salt marsh, but their numbers are swelled in winter with many migrants arriving from the north.

Often called "the sentinel of the marsh", they are quick to call the alarm at approaching danger, both human and avian. A first sight of a bird of prey they fly up calling loudly and revealing the white trailing edge of the wings and a white V up the back.

15

Black-headed gull

Only in its spring breeding plumage does this small and gregarious gull have a black, or more correctly dark brown head. The rest of the year there is just a smudge of ash grey on the cheek behind the eye.

Present all year, Black-headed Gulls nest in large colonies on salt marsh islands, safe from land based egg thieves such as foxes and badgers. Here they have sufficient numbers to drive off aerial threats from crows and larger gulls.

Young birds appear in mid-summer and have mottled brown marking which they gradually lose, taking one year to moult into full adult plumage.

16

Common Tern

These elegant "sea swallows" are summer visitors, arriving in early April to fish the creeks and channels along the coast.

Generally white in colour with grey wings and a black cap, they can be mistaken for a gull, but are much more graceful and have a narrow red bill with a black tip.

Common Terns nest on shingle ridges both on the coast and inland along rivers, lakes and gravel pits. Late summer will often find a pair trailing one or two noisy youngsters constantly begging for food.

These birds are great travellers, leaving our shores in autumn they spent the winter fishing palm fringed lagoons along the African west coast.

17

Reed Bunting

A small seed-eating bird that as its name suggests frequents the reed beds and borrow-dykes that border the estuary.

In spring the males are smartly dressed with a black head and a white collar and moustache, they sing a simple jaunty song from the top of a reed.

The more secretive female is streaked brown with white outer-tail feathers which are constantly flicked; she builds a hair-lined nest hidden in herbage close to the ground.

In winter small flocks will gather to feed on seeds out on the saltmarsh.

18

Kingfisher

A shrill call and a flash of blue disappearing down river is usually all you see of a Kingfisher. Nesting in burrows in the banks of rivers and old gravel pits, Kingfishers move to saltwater creeks in winter to dive for small fish from posts, ropes and buoys.

Despite their bright colours, rich orange breast, blue-green crown and wings, with a gleaming cerulean blue back, they can be surprisingly hard to spot when perched in a quiet corner.